How Gene Therapy Is Changing Society

John Allen

ReferencePoint Press®

San Diego, CA

About the Author
John Allen is a writer living in Oklahoma City.

© 2016 ReferencePoint Press, Inc.
Printed in the United States

For more information, contact:
ReferencePoint Press, Inc.
PO Box 27779
San Diego, CA 92198
www. ReferencePointPress.com

LIBRARY OF CONGRESS CATALOGING-IN-PUBLICATION DATA

Allen, John, 1957- author.
  How gene therapy is changing society / by John Allen.
    pages cm. -- (Science, technology, and society series)
  Audience: Grades 9 to 12
  Includes bibliographical references and index.
  ISBN-13: 978-1-60152-898-8 (hardback)
  ISBN-10: 1-60152-898-1 (hardback)
  1. Gene therapy--Juvenile literature. 2. Medical technology--Moral and ethical aspects--Juvenile literature. 3. Medical technology--Social aspects--Juvenile literature. 4. Medical ethics--Juvenile literature. I. Title.
  RB155.8.A45 2015
  615.8'95--dc23
                                                                    2014048807

Contents

"Science and technology have had a major impact on society, and their impact is growing. By drastically changing our means of communication, the way we work, our housing, clothes, and food, our methods of transportation, and, indeed, even the length and quality of life itself, science has generated changes in the moral values and basic philosophies of mankind.

"Beginning with the plow, science has changed how we live and what we believe. By making life easier, science has given man the chance to pursue societal concerns such as ethics, aesthetics, education, and justice; to create cultures; and to improve human conditions. But it has also placed us in the unique position of being able to destroy ourselves."

— Donald P. Hearth, former director of the
NASA Langley Research Center, 1985.

Donald P. Hearth wrote these words in 1985. They appear in the foreword of a publication titled *The Impact of Science on Society*, a collection of speeches given during a public lecture series of the same name. Although Hearth's words were written about three decades ago, they are as true today as when they first appeared on the page.

Advances in science and technology undeniably bring about societal change. Gene therapy, for instance, has the potential to revolutionize medicine and the treatment of debilitating illnesses such as sickle-cell anemia and Parkinson's disease. Medical experts say gene therapy might also be used to treat conditions ranging from obesity to depression and someday, perhaps, even to help extend human life spans.

Although gene therapy offers great hope and promise, it also carries significant risks. The 1999 death of an eighteen-year-old patient taking part in a gene therapy clinical trial in the United States provided a painful reminder of the need for strict safeguards and monitoring. Other risks may be less tangible for the time being, but they are no less serious. The idea of changing the genetic instructions for human beings can be construed in some instances as arrogant, immoral, and dangerous. The possibility of making such changes raises questions of who should decide which traits are normal and desirable and which are to be considered unhealthy. It raises questions about the enhancement of the intellectual and athletic capabilities of individuals and about the potential for discrimination against those judged to be in possession of less desirable or faulty genes.

ReferencePoint's *Science, Technology, and Society* series examines scientific and technological advances in the context of their impact on society. Topics covered in the series include gene therapy, the Internet, renewable energy, robotics, and mobile devices. Each book explores how and why this science or technology came about; how it has influenced or shaped daily life and culture; efforts to guide or control the technology through laws and policies; and what the next generation of this technology might look like. Included in the chapters are focus questions aimed at eliciting conversation and debate. Also included are key words and terms and their meanings in the context of the topics covered. Fully documented quotes enliven the narrative and add to the usefulness of the series as a tool for student researchers.

The study of science, technology, and society—sometimes referred to as STS—has gained significant ground in recent years. Top universities, including Stanford and UC Berkeley in California and MIT and Harvard in Massachusetts, are among the many that offer majors or specialized programs devoted to the study of science, technology, and society. The National Science Foundation, an independent federal agency created by Congress in 1950, even has a program that funds research and education specifically on this topic. For secondary students interested in this field, or for those who are merely curious or just trying to fulfill an assignment, ReferencePoint's new series can provide a useful and accessible starting point.

1985
W. French Anderson and others use a retrovirus vector to deliver working genes to cells with adenosine deaminase deficiency.

1977
Frederick Sanger develops a technique for rapid sequencing of DNA, allowing for the identification of genetic mutations.

1972
Paul Berg constructs the first human-altered DNA molecule, combining genes from different organisms.

1969
Werner Arber, Hamilton O. Smith, and Daniel Nathans discover restriction enzymes, which can cut DNA at specific locations.

1941
George W. Beadle and Edward L. Tatum repair a gene defect by adding a missing enzyme to a microorganism.

1970
Stanfield Rogers conducts the first gene therapy trial on two sisters in Germany.

1976
The National Institutes of Health in the United States produces guidelines for research on genetic modification.

1953
James D. Watson and Francis Crick publish a scientific paper describing the double helix structure of the DNA molecule.

2000
Several French boys develop leukemia in a gene therapy trial, resulting in more reports of gene therapy's failure. Regulations on gene therapy research are increased in Europe and the United States.

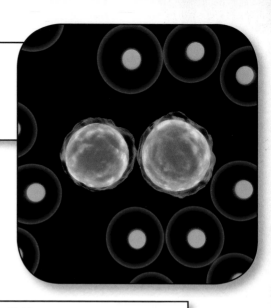

1990
W. French Anderson and colleagues perform successful gene therapy on four-year-old Ashanti DeSilva, drawing worldwide acclaim.

1999
Eighteen-year-old Jesse Gelsinger dies in a clinical trial for gene therapy, bringing research to a virtual halt.

2012
The medical agency of the European Union approves Glybera for marketing in Europe, making it the first gene therapy product to be marketed in the West.

2003
The Chinese State Food and Drug Administration approves the commercial production of Gendicine, making it the world's first gene therapy drug to reach the market.

2014
Feng Zhang receives a US patent for CRISPR, a tool for editing strands of DNA that shows tremendous promise for the future.

2005
James M. Wilson, who led the gene therapy trial in which Jesse Gelsinger died, helps develop adeno-associated viruses for use as vectors in gene therapy.

A Promising Success

At first the Warnells of Maidenhead, England, were pleased their five-week-old baby, Nina, was sleeping through the night. But her lack of appetite began to worry them. Soon Nina grew ill, first with a rotavirus infection, then with pneumonia. In March 2012 doctors discovered that Nina had a genetic defect that caused her to be born without an immune system. With no defenses against disease, Nina seemed fated to live as a "bubble child," cut off from the world in a sterile environment. "The doctors said 'you need to prepare yourself for the fact that Nina probably isn't going to survive,'"[1] recalls Nina's father, Graeme.

More than two years later, however, Nina not only is still alive, she plays with visitors and even enjoys strolls in the park with her mother, Aga. She has a functioning immune system that continues to grow stronger. As Graeme says, "We have gone from facing losing a daughter to having the family back."[2] And she owes her new life to a medical treatment called gene therapy.

Gene therapy is the technique of curing disease or improving the body's ability to fight disease by replacing a faulty gene or adding a healthy gene. This approach is the product of decades of research into DNA and how genes operate. Genes are tiny sections of the DNA molecule that determine the characteristics of an organism. They are like the instructions for every living thing. As genes are passed from one generation to the next, they are constantly changing. This process of change, called mutation, can also result in disruptions of normal gene activity. Mutation can cause diseases such as cancer or physical defects like Nina Warnell's lack of a working immune system. In fact, medical researchers have discovered many diseases and disabilities that are the result of faulty genes. Using special screening techniques, researchers are able to identify and target problem genes for replacement or correction. Many medical experts believe gene therapy has the potential to revolutionize medicine and the treatment of illness. It may also be used to treat a variety of conditions from obesity to depression. Someday gene therapy might even help increase human life spans.

Drawbacks and Safety Concerns

For all its potential, however, gene therapy is still in the experimental stage. Predictions that it would be the magical cure for many different diseases and disabilities proved premature. Researchers have found the connections between genetics and disease to be much more complex than they anticipated. For example, instead of being the sole cause of a disease, genes may only make an individual more susceptible. Genetic triggers may be set off by environmental factors such as stress, pollution, or smoking. Researchers have also faced challenges finding safe methods to deliver gene therapy to patients. Treatment generally involves using a virus as a delivery agent—called a vector—to introduce new or modified genes to certain cells. However, physicians must choose among a bewildering array of viruses to find the best one for a specific condition. The virus must target the correct cells, integrate the gene into the cells, and avoid harmful side effects to the patient. Researchers have found that accomplishing all this is a delicate balancing act.

> **immune system**
>
> The system of structures and processes in the body that protect against disease.

Concerns about the safety of gene therapy continue to dog its progress. Because the treatment is relatively new, its risks are still coming to light. Serious risks to patients include inflammation, toxic effects, and cancer. Widespread optimism about gene therapy in the 1990s was derailed by the death in 1999 of an eighteen-year-old American patient taking part in a clinical trial. The incident led the US Food and Drug Administration (FDA) and the National

Chromosomes, Genes, and DNA

The human body is made up of trillions of cells, and inside each cell is the nucleus. The nucleus contains forty-six chromosomes—or twenty-three pairs. The chromosomes consist of thousands of genes. The genes are made up of DNA. DNA holds the blueprint for how living organisms are built. It has a ribbonlike structure that looks like two long, twisted strands when it is not in its usual condensed form. Genes play an essential role in the human body. They encode instructions for making proteins, which are critical to helping the body grow, work properly, and remain healthy. Genes are also involved in the repair of damaged cells and tissues. But when genes themselves are damaged or changed—or mutated—they cease to function properly. This can lead to illness, which is why gene therapy is of so much interest to scientists.

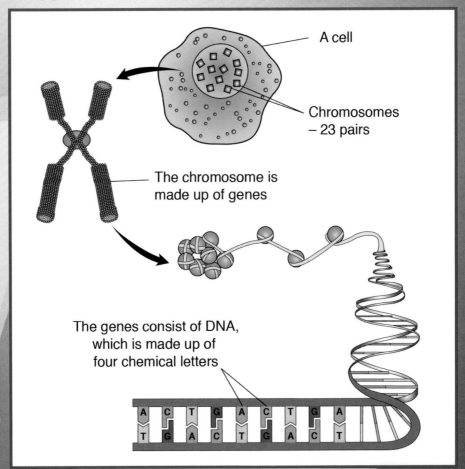

A cell

Chromosomes – 23 pairs

The chromosome is made up of genes

The genes consist of DNA, which is made up of four chemical letters

A C T G A C T G A
T G A C T G A C T

Source: Abramson Cancer Center of the University of Pennsylvania, "Gene Therapy: The Basics," September 7, 2010. www.oncolink.org.

Institutes of Health to suspend other trials and set up new programs for protecting patients in gene therapy research. The result was a much more cautious approach among both regulators and research staff. Studies were closely monitored for safeguards. As of 2014 no human gene therapy product has won FDA approval for sale in the United States, and only one is available in Europe.

Ethical Issues

Aside from mixed practical results, gene therapy also faces ethical concerns. Changing the genetic instructions for human beings strikes some observers as immoral and dangerous. Tampering with genes, they warn, could have unforeseen consequences for the human species. Questions arise as to who will decide which traits are normal and desirable and which are to be considered unhealthy. The possibility of using gene therapy to create people who are intellectually or athletically enhanced is no longer confined to science fiction. People with genes judged to be faulty could face discrimination or pressure to submit to therapy. These and other ethical issues only increase the perception that gene therapy research should proceed with caution.

mutation

A permanent change in the DNA sequence within an organism.

Despite its fitful progress today, the future of gene therapy remains bright. Successes so far have been limited and have mostly dealt with obscure diseases that afflict few individuals. Yet evidence from patients such as Nina Warnell shows that the technology works, and many biotech companies are investing large sums on the development of new treatments. In fact, the next big question may be the high price of gene therapy. "The advances in the science of gene therapy are thrilling," says Matt Patterson, the CEO of a San Francisco–based biotech company, "but we also need to begin to think about how to implement these things into the health-care system if we're successful."[3] Society must decide who will pay for expensive treatments and whether they should be available to everyone. With its enormous potential—and undeniable hazards— gene therapy promises to be controversial for years to come.

The Origin of Gene Therapy

"The ideal treatment for genetic disorders would be a form of genetic alteration, a correction of the genes that cause the problem. And the benefit of such gene therapy would last the patient's whole life; once fixed, it's fixed for good."

—James D. Watson, Nobel Prize–winning geneticist and codiscoverer of the structure of DNA.

James D. Watson, *DNA: The Secret of Life*. New York: Knopf, 2003, p. 349.

—————————————

Gene therapy owes its beginnings to a breakthrough in molecular biology more than sixty years ago. In 1953 two scientists published a one-page paper in a British scientific weekly called *Nature*. The paper, blandly titled "A Structure for Deoxyribose Nucleic Acid," drew little attention at first. The authors of the paper flipped a coin to decide whose name would appear first, James D. Watson winning out over Francis Crick. Crick's wife, Odile, contributed a schematic drawing of the double helix structure that the authors had discovered for DNA, which is the molecule that contains all the genetic information about an organism. The paper suggested that DNA's double spiral ladder form was key to its ability to produce exact copies of itself and pass on genetic traits. Before publication, Crick had told his wife that he and Watson seemed to have made an important discovery, but she was initially unimpressed. "You were always coming home and saying things like that, so naturally I thought nothing of it,"[4] she said. Actually, Watson and Crick's description of the DNA molecule was a great milestone of twentieth-century science and was destined to have a profound effect on society and on human beings' ideas about themselves and the natural world.

Recombinant DNA Research

Years before Watson and Crick's discovery of the double helix, scientists knew that genes contain instructions for making proteins, which in turn are the building blocks of life. Each gene in DNA creates a hereditary characteristic that corresponds to a single protein. It took scientists more than a decade after Watson and Crick's breakthrough to figure out the exact correspondence between nucleotides in DNA and amino acids in proteins. This is the relationship that defines the genetic code.

As scientists unlocked the secrets of the genetic code, some speculated about how DNA could be artificially recombined. For eons, nature has constantly created new combinations of DNA. Now it seemed possible to do the same thing in a laboratory. Key to this research was the discovery of restriction enzymes in 1970. Restriction enzymes are found in bacteria, where they act as a rudimentary immune system. A restriction enzyme protects a bacterium from an invading virus by chopping up the virus's DNA so that it cannot replicate. The restriction enzyme restricts, or limits, the ability of bacterial viruses to infect their host. Molecular biologists Werner Arber, Hamilton O. Smith, and Daniel Nathans found that restriction enzymes are able to cut DNA at precise locations in order to isolate fragments that contain genes. "We knew immediately we had a restriction enzyme," says Smith, describing the breakthrough. "Because it was an enzyme that was recognizing—somehow it was reading sequences, it knew that this was another DNA of some sort."[5] The trio's discovery of these biological scissors earned them the 1978 Nobel Prize in Physiology or Medicine. Scientists went on to isolate more than four thousand different restriction enzymes from a vast range of bacterial strains. These provide a varied toolbox for manipulating genes.

molecular biology

The branch of biology that deals with the structure and function of molecules such as DNA, RNA, and proteins.

In their Cambridge University laboratory in 1953, James D. Watson (left) and Francis Crick (right) use a large model to explain their momentous discovery of the structure of DNA. The field of gene therapy owes its beginnings to this scientific breakthrough.

Restriction enzymes opened up a new world of research into recombinant DNA, also called rDNA or genetic engineering. Suddenly, it was possible to cut and paste strands of DNA and introduce new combinations of genetic material. According to American biochemist Paul Berg, "That is the critical step, the recognition that you could take a complex mixture of a million different pieces of DNA and separate them physically one from another by putting them into a bacterial cell and allow the bacteria to amplify them. That's the origin of recombinant DNA . . . the ability to cut pieces of DNA up with restriction enzymes."[6] In 1972 Berg constructed the first human-altered DNA molecule, combining genes from different organisms. A few years later British scientist Frederick Sanger developed a technique for rapid sequencing of strands of DNA—that is, a method of reading the exact order of nucleotides in a molecule of DNA. This helped researchers determine which segments of DNA contain genes and identify changes in genetic sequence, called mutations. Sanger's work led to a worldwide effort to map all the genes of the human species—called the genome. The new rDNA technology promised to affect every area of biological research, from medicine to agriculture to law enforcement. By the beginning of the twenty-first century, microbiology began to rival computer science in its potential impact on society and everyday life.

> **nucleotide**
>
> An organic molecule that serves as a building block or subunit of nucleic acids such as DNA and RNA.

Treatment for Hereditary Disease

Some of the most exciting possibilities for rDNA lay in medical research, particularly on hereditary, or genetic-based, diseases. In the 1960s scientists and physicians postulated the use of rDNA technology to replace defective DNA with healthy DNA. This form of treatment became known as gene therapy. In 1970 Dr. Stanfield Rogers of Oak Ridge National Laboratory in Tennessee conducted the first gene therapy trial on humans. Rogers discovered a virus carrying the gene to make arginase, an enzyme that breaks down the amino acid arginine. He read of two sisters in Germany whose hereditary lack of the arginase enzyme caused them to have seizures and mental impairment. Traveling to Cologne, Germany, Rogers worked with German scientists to treat the girls with gene therapy. Rogers's attempt to deliver the healthy gene into the sisters' cells by way of the virus he had discovered proved unsuccessful. The treatment also attracted a great deal of criticism on ethical grounds, as some experts questioned the wisdom of tampering with human genes. Yet the method he and his German colleagues used became one of the basic techniques for future gene therapy.

Another early experiment in gene therapy developed from the work of W. French Anderson and Kenneth Culver of the National Heart, Lung, and Blood Institute and Michael Blaese of the National Cancer Institute. In the mid-1980s the team pursued gene therapy through the use of tissue culture, which involves growing and sustaining body tissue in the laboratory. They studied how genes could be safely transferred into the bone marrow cells in animals using a retrovirus, a virus capable of producing its own DNA when injected into cells. The process was moderately successful but affected too few cells to be useful as a treatment. When the team switched to white blood cells instead of bone marrow cells, the number of corrected genes that spread to other cells in animal experiments was much greater. Encouraged, the team began searching for a way to test its delivery method on a person.

hereditary

Passed down from one generation to the next.

In 1990 Anderson and his colleagues learned of Ashanti DeSilva, a four-year-old girl whose body lacked a gene that produces a protein called adenosine deaminase (ADA), rendering her immune system drastically impaired. With every virus or bacterium a threat to her life, Ashanti had to live at home in a plastic bubble environment, depending on injections of synthetic ADA to survive. Like Nina Warnell, Ashanti faced early death as the injections became less effective over time. With no other options for treatment, Ashanti's parents agreed to submit their daughter to a clinical trial conducted by Anderson's team. Extracting blood cells from Ashanti's veins, the team employed a hollowed-out virus vector to insert healthy copies of the ADA gene into the blood cells. The engineered cells were then injected back into Ashanti's bloodstream. There was no chance of rejection, as with bone marrow transplants, since Ashanti's body recognized the altered cells as her own. The effect of the treatment was dramatic, as Ashanti's immune system immediately grew more active. With-

The Human Genome Project

The discoveries of DNA's double helix structure and techniques for rapid sequencing of DNA led to the Human Genome Project (HGP). This is a worldwide collaborative effort to map and investigate all the genes of human beings, called the genome. The project began in 1988, when the US Congress authorized a detailed analysis of the human genome to protect against mutations resulting from the effects of nuclear radiation. James D. Watson was appointed to lead the new Office of Human Genome Research for the National Institutes of Health. Geneticists and microbiologists in many countries contributed research. Much of the work centered on finding ways to decipher the genome more rapidly. In February 2001 HGP researchers published the first draft of the human genome—90 percent complete—in the scientific journal *Nature*. Experts compared the impact of the project's success to that of the Apollo moon landing. The fully sequenced genome reached completion in 2003.

The HGP was full of surprises. It showed that human genes number about 20,500—far fewer than expected. It also revealed that the mixture of human proteins is merely a more complex arrangement of similar genes in roundworms and fruit flies. Yet the HGP research holds enormous promise in many different fields. According to Francis Collins, the former director of the National Human Genome Research Institute, the genome is "a transformative textbook of medicine, with insights that will give health care providers immense new powers to treat, prevent and cure disease."

Quoted in National Human Genome Research Institute, "What Was the Human Genome Project?," www.genome.gov.

in six months she was able to safely leave her house, and after two years she enrolled in school and embarked on a normal life. With periodic treatments of gene therapy and occasional doses of ADA, Ashanti has maintained sufficient levels of the needed enzyme in her blood.

News reports about Ashanti's case hailed gene therapy as a cure-all for genetic disease. Many scientists were equally enthusiastic. Gene therapy, which had previously been successful only with plants and animals, was shown to be capable of treating hereditary disease in humans. Cancer, hemophilia, sickle-cell anemia—there were so many conditions that might yield to the new treatment. Gene therapy might also replace many forms of drug therapy. "Drugs sent into the body have an effect for a while," says medical author Ramez Naam, "but eventually are broken up or passed out. Gene therapy, on the other hand, gives the body the ability to manufacture the needed protein or enzyme or other chemical itself. The new genes can last for a few weeks or can become a permanent part of the patient's genome."[7] In other words, gene therapy can direct the body's cells to conduct their own repairs.

How Gene Therapy Works

The goal of gene therapy is to insert a normal gene into a cell's chromosome to replace a faulty or dysfunctional gene. First the faulty gene that is causing a disease must be identified. Then the precise location of the cells it affects in the body's organs or tissues must be found. Next a healthy version of the gene must be obtained. To accomplish this, the correct segment of DNA is snipped from the genetic material in a normal cell using a restriction enzyme. All this is a prelude to the really difficult part.

The largest challenge in gene therapy is getting the new gene into the patient's cells. The replacement gene cannot be simply administered like a medicine. It must be delivered using a special carrier called a vector, which is engineered to get the gene to the desired location. The earliest researchers in gene therapy found that viruses were ideal for use as vectors. Viruses such as the common cold penetrate cell walls and introduce their genes into a host cell as part of their replication cycle. Virus genes instruct the cell to produce copies of the virus, causing an increasing number of cells to become infected. Researchers found that hollowed-out viruses could be employed to deliver healthy or undamaged genes into a human cell. When employed as a vector, a virus is first modified by the replacement of its disease-causing genes with the desired good genes. All this must be done while still ensuring that the virus retains the genes necessary for inserting its genetic material into the host. If the therapy is successful, the cell with the new gene will begin to reproduce, replacing faulty genes with healthy ones in billions of cells.

Gene Therapy via Viruses

Viruses provide a remarkably efficient delivery method for gene therapy. Viruses acting as carriers, or vectors, invade cells naturally, can target specific kinds of cells, and can be engineered to replace disease-carrying genes with healthy replacement genes. In gene therapy, the viral vector is genetically altered so that it can deliver healthy or undamaged genes into a human cell and not cause illness. The gene with modified DNA is injected into the viral vector, sometimes packaged in a fluid-filled or air-filled sac called a vesicle. Once the vector is infused or injected into the patient's body, it must bind to the cell membrane. Once inside the cell, the vesicle breaks down and releases the vector. The vector then injects the modified gene into the cell nucleus, where it can begin making the protein needed for whatever treatment doctors are trying to achieve.

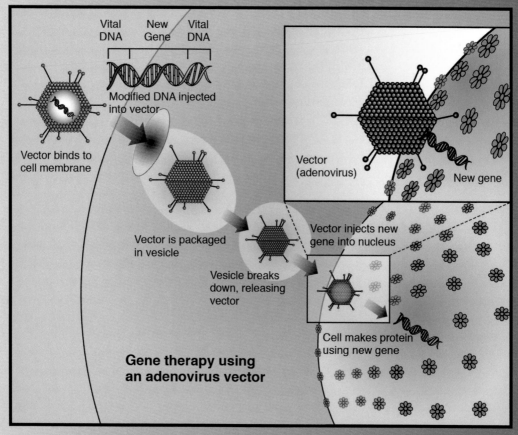

Gene therapy using an adenovirus vector

Source: Abramson Cancer Center of the University of Pennsylvania, "Gene Therapy: The Basics," September 7, 2010. www.oncolink.org.

A related gene therapy technique—as used in Ashanti DeSilva's case—involves removing a sample of a patient's cells, introducing the vector in the laboratory, and returning the treated cells to the patient's body. This method, called *ex vivo* (outside the organism) in contrast to the *in vivo* (inside the organism) technique of injecting the vector into the patient directly, tends to reduce the likelihood of unwanted immune response. In either method, viruses deliver gene therapy through nature's own distribution system.

Suicide Genes to Fight Cancer

Gene therapy can also be used in tandem with other treatments to increase their effectiveness. For example, chemotherapy for cancer can be improved by use of an early form of gene therapy called the suicide gene approach. This method was first proposed in 1986 by Frederick Moolten, a cancer research specialist at Harvard Medical School. In essence, a suicide gene programs cancer cells to eliminate themselves.

This approach is a vast improvement over chemotherapy alone, which has long been the dominant method of cancer treatment. Chemotherapy has crucial limitations, being a fairly blunt instrument when it comes to targeting specific tumor cells. Unlike chemotherapy, suicide gene therapy tailors the treatment to the patient's own tissues. Moolten's original research used a herpes simplex virus as the vector to deliver gene therapy to cancer cells. A gene from the patient's tumor cell is removed and then altered with other genes to create enzymes that are harmless to the patient's healthy cells. The enzymes are injected into the tumor cells using the viral vector. The enzymes then release a prodrug—a form that is only partially active at the start—that causes the cancerous cells to "commit suicide," or destroy themselves, but leaves normal cells unharmed. This ability to distinguish between healthy and cancerous cells is one of the main benefits of suicide gene therapy. While suicide gene therapy does not eliminate the need for chemotherapy, it renders remaining tumor cells more vulnerable to the latter. Suicide gene therapy remains one of the most promising cancer-fighting tools.

Researchers soon discovered that gene therapy cannot always be accomplished by substituting healthy genes for unhealthy genes. Sometimes the function of normal genes is disrupted by a mutation that produces so-called dominant-negative proteins. Simply adding a working copy of the gene does no good because the dominant-negative proteins will still disrupt its operation. Similarly, a gain-of-function mutation can cause normal cells to grow and divide unnaturally, as happens with many cancers. Healthy genes may also be regulated improperly due to some disorder of the body's proteins. In these and other situations, gene therapists must find novel ways to repair the affected gene, turn off or "silence" the unwanted proteins, or block their effects.

vector

The carrier, such as a modified virus, that holds the new gene used in gene therapy.

The Trouble with Vectors

The problem of finding a suitable vector for a gene therapy treatment raises the Goldilocks dilemma: It must be *just right*. Since there is no ideal vector that works for every disorder, each vector must be customized to make it more suitable for a particular treatment. A successful vector must satisfy several requirements. It must be simple to make in very large quantities. One gene therapy treatment may call for billions of copies of the vector in order to reach every cell in the targeted tissue. It must target the correct cells precisely, so that a gene that is needed in the cells of the pancreas does not end up in the lungs. Since gene expression— the process by which genetic instructions direct the creation of particular proteins—is tissue specific, viral vectors must be, too. The vector must also integrate the new gene in the target cells. This means the gene must become part of the genetic material of the host cell so that copies of the cell will also contain the new gene. Finally, the vector must activate the gene, which involves switching on the production of the protein in the host cell's nucleus. The vector must do all this while avoiding dangerous side effects such as unforeseen toxic reactions or the triggering of an immune response against it.

Viruses—or viral vectors—generally have proved to be the most efficient delivery method for gene therapy. Viral vectors invade cells naturally, can target specific kinds of cells, and can be engineered to replace disease-carrying genes with healthy replacement genes. However, viral vectors are not without drawbacks. Since they can hold only limited genetic material, viruses cannot accept larger replacement genes. And despite researchers' best efforts, viral vectors sometimes trigger an unwanted immune response, which can block delivery of the new genes, kill the cells once delivery is complete, or possibly make the patient sick. According to Dr. Jeffrey Isner, a professor of medicine at Tufts University School of Medicine, the early use of viral vectors was ingenious but flawed. "It was a very logical approach," Isner says. "But in most cases the strategy failed, because the vectors we have today are not ready for prime time."[8]

To avoid these problems, nonviral vectors such as plasmids may be used. A plasmid is a circular DNA molecule found in almost all bacteria. Although plasmids do not penetrate into cells and transfer genes as efficiently as viruses, they can carry larger genes and in most cases do not set off an immune response. Gene therapy plasmids sometimes are loaded inside small membrane bubbles called liposomes, which fuse with cell membranes to deliver their genetic contents. Another promising delivery tool for gene therapy is a synthetic vector called a virosome, which is essentially an empty envelope of influenza virus composed of viral proteins. Virosomes combine the efficiency and targeting accuracy of viral vectors with the greater capacity and safety of plasmids. Yet another possible approach is the gene gun, a powerful vacuum pump that delivers DNA to a cell via minuscule balls of gold or tungsten. Shot with the force of bullets from a rifle, the microscopic pellets pierce the cell membrane and release engineered DNA particles for therapy.

A Time of Optimism

In the 1990s newspapers and TV reports suggested that medical research on gene therapy was on the brink of a miraculous cure-all for stubborn diseases. While scientists and physicians

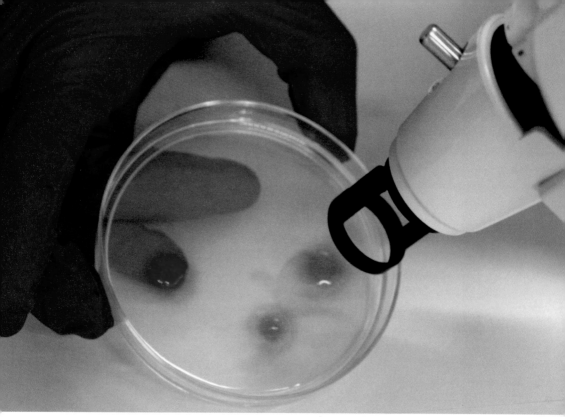

A gene gun bombards the gel-like contents of a petri dish with DNA-coated gold particles. This demonstration shows one possible method of delivering modified DNA to the cells.

remained more cautious, many were intrigued by the possibilities for the new technology. Qualified successes such as Ashanti DeSilva's case led more researchers to conduct clinical trials. Gene therapy treatments for diseases ranging from cystic fibrosis to HIV to various forms of cancer went into development. In 1991 alone, the US government contributed $58 million for gene therapy research, with sizable increases over the next four years. In 1992 Henry Brem, director of neurological oncology at the Johns Hopkins School of Medicine, administered cutting-edge gene therapy treatments to brain cancer patients. "It is very significant not only for treating malignant brain tumors, but it [also] opens up the door to a whole new approach to treating tumors," Brem said at the time. "It is the first step to seeing the fulfillment of gene therapy."[9] The future of gene therapy seemed assured, if not limitless. Yet huge roadblocks—and tough questions—lay just ahead.

Balancing Safety and Research

Focus Questions

1. Do you think the scientists treating Jesse Gelsinger did an adequate job of monitoring patient safety in the trial? Why or why not?
2. Are researchers justified in placing patients in risky clinical trials in order to find out whether a particular therapy works? Explain your answer.
3. Should seriously ill or terminal patients have the option to take risky drugs if they think they have no other options? Why or why not?

"To put it simply, if we cannot guarantee sound research in general—and patients' safety in particular—public support for gene therapy and other potentially lifesaving treatments will evaporate. . . . So clinical researchers and the institutions that support them must, without exception, maintain the public's confidence in our work, our competence, and most important, our ethics."

—Donna Shalala, secretary of the Department of Health and Human Services.

Donna Shalala, "Protecting Research Subjects—What Must Be Done," *New England Journal of Medicine*, September 14, 2000. www.nejm.org.

Enthusiasm for the prospects of gene therapy continued to grow in the 1990s. In 1999 alone, more than one hundred clinical trials for gene therapy won approval. As a result, dissenting voices tended to get lost in the din. Yet some scientists expressed public concerns about the new technology. They noted the deaths of test animals in gene therapy experiments and questioned the speed with which clinical trials on humans were approved. A few criticized the review process used by the Recombinant DNA Advisory Committee (RAC) of the National Institutes of Health. In general, critics emphasized the many failures so far and urged a more cautious approach to gene therapy going forward. Ruth Macklin, a bioethicist and member of the RAC panel that oversaw gene therapy research, said flatly in 1999, "Gene therapy is not yet therapy."[10]

In response, researchers insisted they did exhaustive studies on animals such as mice, rhesus monkeys, and baboons before even thinking about human trials. And they justified moving rapidly because of the urgent needs of terminal patients with genetic disorders.

bioethicist

A person who deals with ethical and moral questions that relate to new technologies and discoveries in biology.

A Sobering Case

In 1999 the booming field of gene therapy research sustained a major setback with the case of Jesse Gelsinger. The eighteen-year-old from Arizona suffered from a rare metabolic disorder called OTC deficiency. This lack of a liver enzyme causes ammonia to build up in the bloodstream. For those with a severe form of the disease, protein-rich foods are deadly: A bite of a hot dog can result in brain damage and coma. Gelsinger's condition, however, was not life threatening. He was able to live a mostly normal life with the help of a low-protein diet and a drug regime of thirty-two pills a day. When he agreed to enter a gene therapy experiment at the University of Pennsylvania, the main reason was to help those afflicted with a fatal form of OTC deficiency. "What's the worst that can happen to me?" he told a friend before he left for the research hospital in Philadelphia. "I die, and it's for the babies."[11]

The ultimate aim of the gene therapy trial, which was conducted at the Institute for Human Gene Therapy at the University of Pennsylvania, was to treat babies born with a severe and fatal form of OTC deficiency. Due to ethical problems about seeking parental consent to perform trials on sick children, the researchers had to settle for adult volunteers who had a milder form of the disease. Gelsinger was one of eighteen people injected with a dose of weakened adenovirus—cold virus. The virus served as a vector containing the working copy of a gene to reverse OTC deficiency. Unlike the other subjects, who handled the injection with few difficulties, Jesse suffered a violent reaction. The virus escaped from his liver cells into his bloodstream, where it migrated to his other organs. This triggered a massive inflammatory response to fight what Jesse's body identified as a dangerous infection. A few hours after his treatment, Gelsinger was running a high fever. He became so bloated with inflammation his family members scarcely recognized him. A chain reaction led from jaundice to abnormally high blood clotting to kidney and lung failure. Four days after the treatment, Gelsinger died.

> **metabolic**
>
> Having to do with the body's metabolism, or system of life-sustaining chemical reactions within cells.

Doctors were baffled as to why Gelsinger had suffered such an extreme reaction to the viral vector. A female patient given the exact same dose of adenovirus had tolerated it with no problem. The researchers speculated that previous exposure to a viral infection might have made Gelsinger's immune system vulnerable to the adenovirus vector. The result was all the more shocking since Gelsinger had seemed such an ideal candidate for the program.

Fallout from the Gelsinger Case

What was certain was that Jesse Gelsinger's death in a clinical trial, especially when he did not suffer from a terminal condition, dealt a devastating blow to gene therapy research. Immediately after his death, the FDA halted the trial, citing an inadequately trained staff and flawed operating procedures. Its subsequent investigation found that Dr. James M. Wilson, the director of the institute, had failed in his obligations as leader of a clinical trial, including the need to keep volunteers properly informed about risks. Donna Shalala, then secretary of the Department of Health and Human Services, declared in the *New England Journal of Medicine*, "This appalling state of affairs is unacceptable."[12]

Gelsinger's family sued the Institute for Human Gene Therapy, claiming its doctors had failed to inform Jesse about possible severe side effects. An investigation revealed that tests of the vector on mice, baboons, and monkeys had resulted in toxic and even fatal side effects, including inflammation. However, the Penn researchers did not consider these effects relevant to the human

Jesse Gelsinger, pictured in a family photo, took part in an experimental gene therapy trial in 1999 as part of an effort to find a treatment for a rare metabolic disorder called OTC deficiency. He died within days of starting the treatment.

A Chinese Milestone

While Jesse Gelsinger's death and other negative events almost brought Western gene therapy to a halt in the early 2000s, Chinese research took a giant step forward. On October 16, 2003, a biotech company in Shenzhen obtained approval from the Chinese government for the world's first commercial gene therapy. The drug, sold under the brand name Gendicine, treats a cancer of the head and neck known to affect about 10 percent of China's 2.5 million new cancer patients each year. Gendicine is delivered via an adenoviral vector and is used mostly in tandem with chemotherapy. Results from trials showed almost two-thirds of patients experienced complete regression of late-stage tumors. According to Zhaohui Peng, the CEO of SiBono, the company that manufactures Gendicine, the therapy's only side effect in five years of clinical trials was minor fever.

Observers in the United States and elsewhere in the West were surprised by the news. Generally, Chinese regulators do not consent to drugs that have not first received approval by Western boards. Critics claimed that the regulatory process in China is much more lax. Other experts suggested that without high-profile failures like the Gelsinger case, Chinese authorities were more receptive to new treatments. "In China, where hundreds of thousands die of diseases such as cancer without access to the clinical options available to patients in the US and Europe, the potential for a one-time treatment that is relatively simple to administer is very appealing," says Mark Kay, a gene therapy researcher at Stanford University.

Quoted in Sue Pearson et al., "China Approves First Gene Therapy," *Nature Biotechnology,* 2004. www.nature.com.

trials since the animals had received much higher doses of the viruses. In January 2000 the FDA stopped the remainder of the human gene therapy trials at the institute and began to investigate almost seventy trials elsewhere in the United States. The FDA also announced two new programs to enhance patient safety. The Gene Therapy Clinical Trial Monitoring Plan set up new requirements for disclosure and safety monitoring before a trial could proceed. It also forbade research team members from owning equity or stock options in any company sponsoring the trial. This provision addressed the fact that Wilson, who headed the institute, owned stock in Genovo, a biotech company that helped finance its gene therapy trials. Another new program, the Gene Transfer Safety Symposia, directed researchers to share data and clinical details, especially with regard to negative results. For the Gelsingers' attorney, nationally known insurance litigator Alan Milstein, such measures still were inadequate. "We are at the crossroads," Milstein said in 2001. "It remains to be seen whether there will be a terrific change or another death. My prediction is another death, because to date there have been no changes that would have prevented Jesse's death."[13]

A further blow to gene therapy's prospects followed an apparent success. In 2000 twenty infant boys in France and the United Kingdom were treated for a rare and fatal condition called X-linked severe combined immune deficiency (SCID-X1, *X* referring to the X chromosome)—a disease like the one afflicting Ashanti DeSilva. Initially, there was optimism, as gene therapies enabled most of the boys to develop functioning immune systems. However, a few years later five of the twenty developed leukemia, a reaction linked to the retroviral vector they had received. This led to more calls for improving the safety of clinical trials and more reports on the failure of gene therapy. Such adverse events caused "a big negative impact in the field,"[14] recalls cell biologist Mien-Chie Hung of the University of Texas MD Anderson Cancer Center. Lost in all the negativity was the fact that the boys probably would have died from immune deficiency had they not received treatment. Although one of the boys did succumb to leukemia, the other four received chemotherapy and now lead remarkably normal lives. Still, the outlook for gene therapy research continued to be bleak in the early 2000s.

Safety Concerns and Complications

Following these setbacks, interest in gene therapy waned. Evidence from clinical trials revealed potential safety issues related to vectors that seemed insurmountable. First, there is the risk of the patient's immune system attacking the introduced virus as an intruder, leading to inflammation and, in extreme instances, organ failure. This is the complication that caused Jesse Gelsinger's death. Second, there is the possibility of the vector targeting the wrong cells. Viruses can act on more than one cell type, so engineered viruses may infect healthy cells as well as the ones with defective genes they are targeting. This can cause serious damage to healthy cells, including diseases such as cancer. Third, the viral vector can sometimes regain its disease-causing ability once it is injected into the body, thus negating its value as medicine. Fourth, there is the chance of inserting replacement genes in the wrong location in the DNA, causing mutations or cancers, as occurred with some of the boys in the SCID-X1 trials. Finally, there is a slight risk of a viral vector delivering new genes to cells involved in reproduction, which could pass on genetic changes to the patient's offspring.

With these risk factors in mind, government agencies in the United States and elsewhere in the world set up tougher guidelines for gene therapy research, particularly in moving from trials on animals to humans. On February 2, 2000, Dr. Jay P. Siegel, director of the Office of Therapeutics Research and Review, testified before Congress about rules to halt research:

> I would like to express . . . our continued concern that gene therapy studies be as safe as possible. . . . Part of the FDA's review of the IND [introduction of new drugs] includes a review of the sponsor's proposed or FDA's recommended stopping rules. The stopping rules are rules in the protocol which assure that a clinical trial will be stopped if certain adverse events should occur.[15]

Along with all the safety concerns, prospects for gene therapy were further complicated by findings that more common disorders such as heart disease and cancer involve not a single gene but several genes on various chromosomes. In many cases simply identifying the correct gene to target was a much greater challenge than originally thought. All these factors contributed to the general malaise in the field of gene therapy. In the early years of the new century, biotech companies that quite recently had been the darlings of Wall Street suddenly found their funding drying up. Once-promising programs shut down, and many microbiologists looked elsewhere for research opportunities.

Signs of a Comeback

Perhaps no scientist's career better exemplifies the highs and lows of gene therapy research than that of James M. Wilson, the founder and director of the Penn Institute for Human Gene Therapy. Wilson's work as a young scientist linked his interest in rare genetic-based diseases to the growing field of gene therapy. In the early 1990s Wilson developed a viral vector to treat a disease related to high levels of LDL, or so-called bad cholesterol. His encouraging success in a human trial led to his being named to the directorship of the new Penn Institute, managing a research staff of more than two hundred. Testing vectors for delivery of gene therapy, Wilson and his staff thought they had found an ideal candidate in adenovirus. The outcome instead was Jesse Gelsinger's death—a catastrophe that seemed to spell doom not only for Wilson's future in genetic research, but for the whole field

adenovirus

The type of virus used in weakened form as a vector in gene therapy.

Scientists have found that adeno-associated viruses (pictured) can be used to deliver genes to the cells without triggering an immune response in the patient. This discovery revitalized gene therapy as a treatment for certain conditions.

The Penn Vector Core

For microbiologists seeking a promising vector for gene therapy research, there is now a site for one-stop shopping. In 2005 James M. Wilson and his colleagues at the University of Pennsylvania's gene therapy program set up a marketplace for viral vectors, the Penn Vector Core. The operation is based on the team's success at finding new adeno-associated viruses (AAVs) in monkeys and humans. Most of the AAVs they have discovered were previously unknown, and many show promise as vectors—or delivery agents—for gene therapy. The viruses are catalogued according to their affinities for certain tissues, improving researchers' ability to target the eyes, the liver, muscle tissue, and so forth. The inventory catalog lists vectors in amounts ranging from small to routine to mega.

The Penn Vector Core makes vectors available—at cost—for scientists around the world. For example, it was a Penn vector that British researchers used in breakthrough clinical trials of a gene therapy treatment for hemophilia. Wilson and his team also work with scientists to design and produce custom vectors suited to the needs of a particular trial. For James M. Wilson, the operation is a fitting tribute to Jesse Gelsinger, the young man who died in a gene therapy trial at the Penn Institute for Human Gene Therapy in 1999. "That tragic event forced me to reevaluate where we were and where the field was," Wilson says. "For this field to succeed, we had to go back to basics. I do believe this is a positive legacy to that."

Quoted in Marie McCullough, "Gene Breakthrough After Sad Setback," Philly.com, November 20, 2012. http://articles.philly.com.

of gene therapy. With his team scattered and his work discredited, Wilson faced lawsuits and a five-year FDA ban on clinical trials on humans. He might have quit science entirely if not for the influence of his mentor, former University of Michigan professor Tachi Yamada, an expert in the field. Wilson admits, "He encouraged me, Tachi did, to make sure that we figure out how to do it right."[16]

Bolstered by a research grant from a biotech company for which Yamada worked, Wilson and some colleagues searched for improved vectors. Their focus was on vectors that would avoid a potentially fatal immune response. They noted that adeno-associated viruses (AAVs)—stealthy viruses that appear next to adenoviruses in cultures from sick patients—seemed to infect cells without causing any known disease. Team member Guangping Gao found a method of rapidly isolating dozens of AAVs, all of which delivered genes effectively without triggering an immune response. Tests showed that each AAV was adapted to treat specific types of tissue. For example, a vector dubbed AAV8 delivered gene therapy to the liver with spectacular efficiency. Almost alone among known vectors, AAV9 could reach a patient's brain through the bloodstream.

By 2005 Wilson's resurgent team at the Penn Institute had identified about three hundred new AAVs and carefully charted the characteristics of half of them. A once-moribund field sprang back to life. As for Wilson, he is quick to express his gratitude to the patient whose death nearly ended all hopes for gene therapy. "The successes happening now are a legacy of Jesse's death," Wilson says. "We *had* to succeed."[17] Lili Wang, one of Wilson's colleagues, has honored Gelsinger in another way—by developing a safer vector, based on AAV8, to treat OTC deficiency.

> **adeno-associated virus (AAV)**
>
> A virus that infects humans but does not cause disease and elicits only a mild immune response.

Promising Treatments for Hemophilia and Hereditary Blindness

The emergence of AAVs has revitalized gene therapy treatments for a number of conditions besides autoimmune disorders. In 2011 researchers in the United Kingdom announced exciting results from a trial involving patients with hemophilia B. Hemophilia is an inherited blood disease in which a patient's blood is unable to clot efficiently. Six patients with the blood disorder received injections of AAV8 virus containing the working gene for the missing clotting factor. A single treatment increased the patients' clotting ability significantly, with four of the subjects able to discontinue their former replacement therapy entirely. Critics point out the improvement in the patients' clotting factor still left their levels well below normal, and subsequent trials have failed to match the success of the UK experiments. Nevertheless, there is renewed optimism, based on the rapid development of new vectors, regarding practical gene-based cures for hemophilia.

Even more exciting is the progress being made on gene therapy to treat blindness. With the eye less sensitive to immune-response problems, virus injections for treatment of eye disorders have caused no serious side effects. And the results of numerous clinical trials are among the most positive for any form of gene therapy. In a trial at the University of Florida, fifteen patients with a rare degenerative disease of the retina were treated with a modified AAV. It produced a form of vitamin A enabling rods and cones—the retina's light receptors— to function. The patients experienced enormous increases in sensitivity to light and ability to read lines on an eye chart. According to molecular virologist William Hauswirth, who led the Florida trial, it will be a few years before such eye therapies are ready for the market. But so far the results are "bordering on spectacular as far as improving vision in the patients."[18]

Gene Therapy Comes to Market

Overall, advances in AAVs and other modified vectors are allowing new clinical trials to address everything from heart disease to muscular dystrophy and cystic fibrosis to nicotine addiction. This renaissance in gene therapy research has also resulted in the first commercial versions of the technology. On November 2, 2012, the medical agency of the European Union announced that the gene therapy product Glybera could be marketed in member nations—making Glybera the first gene therapy drug approved for use in the West. Glybera is used to treat a rare inherited disorder in which a lack of lipoprotein lipase (LPL), an enzyme that breaks down fats, causes patients to have severe attacks of pancreatitis. Glybera employs an AAV to deliver its working copy of LPL genes into muscle cells, which then begin producing the enzyme on their own.

Tomas Salmonson, chair of the Committee for Medicinal Products for Human Use, acknowledged that the approval process was difficult. According to Salmonson:

> Our established ways of assessing the benefits and risks of Glybera were challenged by the extreme rarity of the

Cells are cultured for use in producing the gene therapy drug Glybera, the first such drug approved for use in the West. The drug, developed by a Dutch company, is used to treat a rare but dangerous enzyme deficiency.

condition and also by uncertainties associated with data provided. In close cooperation with the CAT [Committee for Advanced Therapies], we have worked out a way to ensure robust and close follow-up of the quality, safety and efficacy of Glybera while giving patients who have to live with this rare disease access to medical treatment.[19]

Although it took time and a mountain of cash to obtain final approval, the head of the Amsterdam-based biotech firm that developed Glybera remains hopeful about the field. "The world has been watching very skeptically, questioning if a gene therapy could ever be approved at all," says Jörn Aldag, CEO of uniQure BV. "We are now at the beginning of a significant growth path for the gene therapy market."[20] The next step is to win FDA approval for Glybera in the United States. That would be the ultimate vindication for the scientist behind the engineered vector—dubbed AAV1— that made Glybera possible: James M. Wilson.

Chapter Three

The Ethics of Gene Therapy

Focus Questions

1. Do you think patients can be adequately informed about the risks of a complicated new procedure such as gene therapy? Why or why not?
2. What effect, if any, would changing human genes involved in reproduction have on future generations? Explain your answer.
3. Should athletes be able to enhance their performance capabilities with gene therapy? Why or why not?

"The gene pool is not owned by anyone. It is the joint property of society. And when you manipulate the gene pool, before one attempts to do that, one needs the agreement of society."

—W. French Anderson, director of the University of Southern California's Gene Therapy Laboratory.

Quoted in Rick Weiss, "Engineering the Unborn," *Washington Post*, March 22, 1998. www.washingtonpost.com.

It is not often that a hardheaded research scientist uses terms such as *jaw-dropping* and *game-changing* to describe a new technology. Only a special sort of breakthrough elicits this kind of enthusiasm, but the gene therapy approach called CRISPR fits the bill. CRISPR—the name is an acronym for clustered regularly interspaced short palindromic repeat—enables scientists to edit genes with a great deal more precision than ever before. The approach is faster and easier than previous techniques for modifying DNA and could make the use of viral vectors seem downright clumsy. Its potential to treat genetic disorders such as Down syndrome and sickle-cell anemia is enormous, not to mention the possible applications for infectious diseases such as HIV. According to the American micro-biologist and Nobel Prize winner Craig Mello, "It's a tremendous breakthrough with huge implications for molecular genetics. It's a real game-changer. It's one of those things that you have to see to believe. I read the scientific papers like everyone else but when I saw it working in my own lab, my jaw dropped. A total novice in my lab got it to work."[21]

CRISPR

A recently discovered microbial system capable of editing strands of DNA with incredible precision.

Like anything associated with gene therapy, however, the new technique does not lack for controversy. Its incredibly pre-cise cutting enzymes allow for editing spe-cific parts of the human genome as efficiently as fixing a misspelling in a line of text on a word processor. CRISPR can even repair gene defects in human embryos conceived through in vitro fertilization. This kind of gene therapy on sperm, eggs, or embryos is current-ly banned in almost every nation. Critics stress the possibility of unintended consequences that could harm future generations. In fact, CRISPR elicits the same debates that have attached to gene therapy since its invention—debates about the ethics of altering human genes.

Ethical Opposition to Gene Therapy

The first opponents of gene therapy on ethical grounds mostly assumed that the technology would advance much more rap-idly than it has. Some of the radical scenarios they envisioned about reckless manipulation of human genes and the creation of designer babies never came to pass, for a variety of reasons such as unforeseen technical challenges. Nevertheless, many of their objections to gene therapy still resonate today. Of course, safety has been a crucial issue from the beginning. Critics raised

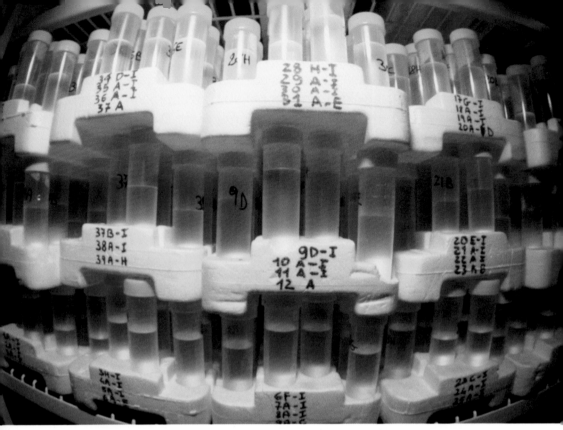

Test tubes containing the entire human genome—that is, all the DNA contained in a human cell—are stored in a laboratory. Early opponents of gene therapy feared the creation of designer babies through the reckless manipulation of genes.

questions about patient rights and informed consent, which is the idea that a person cannot make a rational decision about a procedure unless he or she is fully apprised of all the potential risks and benefits. With an experimental procedure like gene therapy in which outcomes are unknown, informed consent becomes all the more difficult to achieve. As gene therapy went from animal trials to human experiments, many observers thought the technology was moving too fast. Critics even accused scientists of using the plight of sick children to justify their haste in using the treatment on humans. "I don't think family desperation is any rationale for doing something stupid,"[22] said Dusty Miller, himself an early gene therapy researcher at the Fred Hutchinson Cancer Research Center in Seattle, Washington.

Other critics approach the issue from a religious viewpoint. They see tampering with human genes as sinful, a dangerous interference with God's creation, like a Dr. Frankenstein taking science too far. In 1984, for example, a group of seventy-five religious leaders led by the political activist Jeremy Rifkin unsuccessfully stumped for a US Senate resolution that would have banned gene therapy permanently. More recently, religious writers have tended to approach the controversy over gene therapy in a more balanced way that avoids fearmongering. They weigh the ethical responsibility to relieve suffering among current and future generations with the need to preserve the genetic heritage that makes human beings what they are. Many religious critics agree that gene therapy has value, but they urge caution and prudence going forward. As an editorial on the Church of Scotland website points out:

> In the late 1960s, leading geneticists showed a remarkable sense of responsibility and humility in organizing a temporary, voluntary moratorium on certain aspects of their research, while the certain risks and problems were assessed. . . . There is an urgent need to develop this sense within [today's] research community—where ethical acuteness does not often match the technical skills, and where constant pressures for recognition or promotion, the need to maintain funding, and simply becoming immersed in research for its own sake, can lead to unthinking science.[23]

Another major ethical concern involves eugenics, a discredited idea of improving the human gene pool by selective breeding. These critics question who gets to decide which kinds of gene therapy are good and desirable and which are not. They fear that the ability to cure inherited disease could also be used to eliminate unwanted human traits of any kind or even to make people taller or more intelligent—an objection usually filed under genetic engineering. In addition, there is the question of consent among future generations. A grandchild may deplore a gene therapy treatment—no matter how well intended—that has resulted in his or her inheritance of altered genes. When a treatment decision affects individuals not yet born, critics insist, it must be made with all the more care.

eugenics

A policy of improving the human genome through selective breeding and sterilization.

Somatic and Germ Line Gene Therapy

The chance of passing on genetic changes to a patient's descendants continues to present an ethical minefield for researchers in gene therapy. The controversy involves two different approaches to the treatment: somatic and germ line. Somatic gene therapy addresses body tissue cells, not reproductive cells. The patient receives an improved or healthy gene to replace one with a mutation, but the change is not passed on to the next generation. The patient's offspring would have the same chance of getting the disease as they would have if no therapy had been done. Should the genetic-based disease reappear in the next generation, gene-replacement therapy would have to be repeated. Somatic gene therapy is the version being performed today.

somatic

Having to do with body tissue cells.

By contrast, germ line gene therapy modifies either germ cells (also called gametes), which are egg or sperm cells, or a zygote, which is a single-cell organism that results from fertilization, or the merging of germ cells. As Professor Robert A. Weinberg of the Massachusetts Institute of Technology explains, "An altered [somatic] gene in your liver or brain may give you cancer, but it has no chance of being passed on to your descendants. Change a [germ line] gene in the sperm or egg, and the possibility looms that your kids will inherit it."[24] Since every cell descends from the fertilized egg, germ line gene therapy enables the transfer of genetic changes to future generations. Indeed, passing on the changes is the whole point of germ line therapy. Its proponents tout it as a permanent therapy for all those who inherit a targeted gene. Successful germ line therapy, they argue, could possibly eliminate a genetic disease from entire families. Since some rare genetic illnesses afflict very few people overall—for example, less than one hundred babies in the United States each year are diagnosed with SCID (the so-called bubble baby disease)—it is considered possible that germ line gene therapy could virtually wipe out some diseases.

Nevertheless, the downside of germ line therapy is undeniable. Gene therapy has proved difficult and unpredictable at best, and a mistake in a germ line approach—say, the introduction of a trait for leukemia—would be compounded by affecting not only a current patient but those yet unborn. Instead of eliminating a disease, the therapy could introduce troublesome traits that would not appear in a patient's descendants until years in the future. In a larger

Self-Improvement Through Modified Genes

Futurists are thinkers who make predictions about how technology might affect individuals and societies in the coming years and decades. Futurists have long touted gene therapy and other gene-based technologies that will allow for adding, copying, deleting, and editing strands of DNA with remarkable precision. Today futurists' forecasts about using gene therapy not only to treat disease but also to build a better human no longer seem so far-fetched. Science writers like Maciamo Hay profess an almost giddy optimism:

> Gene therapy is so revolutionary that it could be used to change one's physical appearance or improve physical capabilities and mental faculties. It would be possible to change skin, hair or eye color with a single injection, and change back later, or choose other tones, almost at will. Unlike plastic surgeries, there is no reason to be afraid of not liking the result. Don't like it? Just edit your DNA and get a new injection.

Hay's views fit with a philosophy called transhumanism, the idea that the traditional limits associated with the human condition no longer apply and will soon be transcended. Not surprisingly, many critics reject such notions on ethical grounds. They fear that changing the human genetic makeup is not only morally wrong but could have tragic consequences in the future. They also note that scientists have not been especially successful in fine-tuning complex systems such as the world economy or the environment. For these critics, the futurists and transhumanists lack one crucial trait: humility.

Maciamo Hay, "Improve Your Health, Looks and Intelligence Thanks to Gene Therapy," *Life 2.0* (blog), April 24, 2014. www.vitamodularis.org.

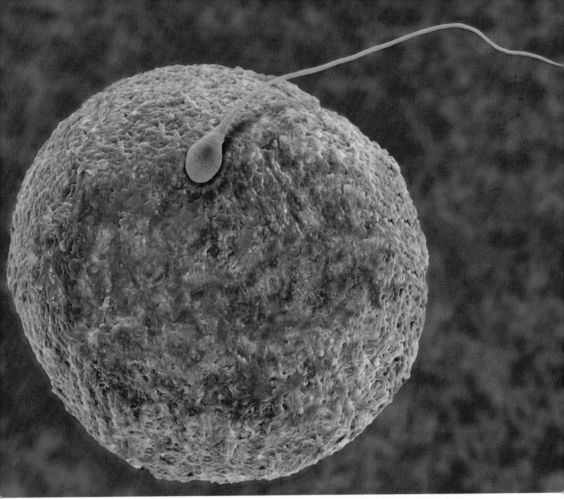

Germ line gene therapy modifies reproductive cells such as those found in the human sperm and egg (pictured in a colored scanning electron micrograph). This form of gene therapy is controversial because it would transfer genetic changes to future generations.

sense, according to the authors of a recent public policy analysis on germ line gene therapy, such experiments "may someday have the ability to alter the trajectory of human evolution."[25]

Today, although scientists continue to debate its value as a treatment and its ethical basis, germ line research is done only on plants and small animals, never on humans. The ethics of somatic versus germ line gene therapy was the subject of a widely discussed editorial in a 1999 issue of the journal *Nature*. "Germline gene therapy and somatic gene therapy are two quite different proposals," wrote the editorialist, "and the legitimate concerns and risks of the former should not be used to stall progress on the latter. The biomedical research community should act quickly and decisively to divorce the two before pushing ahead with . . . somatic gene therapy protocols."[26]

Viral Gene Shedding

Critics of gene therapy note another way that engineered genes can be transferred to the larger population: viral gene shedding. This occurs when the blood or excreta of a gene therapy patient is "shed," or passed on to other people through personal contact or disseminated in the environment. Excreta are body products such as urine, feces, saliva, sweat, and semen. The viruses used as vectors in gene therapy can still retain some infectious ability, though not as much as the parent strain from which they have been derived. Thus, even after a virus has been altered to deliver a therapeutic gene, the chance of it infecting untreated individuals nearby remains. As with any virus, there is always the potential for widespread infection. Currently, there are studies under way to determine how likely it is that engineered viruses and bacteria will spread from human contact or from contact with infected clothing or personal items. Researchers tend to believe that viral vectors, as weakened forms of wild-type strains, are much less infectious and remain infectious for shorter periods. They want to preserve the quality of life for gene therapy patients by allowing them to live in a normal environment and not be sequestered like special cases. Nevertheless, those who oppose gene therapy on ethical grounds see viral gene shedding as one more example of its unpredictable nature. They insist that researchers actually do not know the extent of the safety risks from shedding. Transferring genetic material in this way might be extremely rare. Or it might be as commonplace as blood, sweat, and tears.

> **germ line**
>
> The line of cells from which the germ cells (egg and sperm) are derived.

Gene Therapy for Physical Enhancement

A chronic lack of oxygen in the blood is just the sort of condition that might be treated with gene therapy. A repaired gene that increased blood-oxygen levels for a heart disease sufferer might enable that person to live a more normal life. However, the same genetic change delivered to an athlete might allow for unheard-of levels of endurance in competition. A marathon runner so treated might shatter existing records. As studies of the human genome reveal the specific genes that account for height, strength, muscle efficiency, and other physical characteristics, the possibilities for targeted enhancement by gene therapy increase. The whole concept of athletic training and fair competition could be upended. Just as steroid use helped rewrite the baseball record book, gene therapy, with a few targeted changes here and there, could produce an army of athletes specially equipped to dominate their sport. Perhaps there would be special leagues for the genetically gifted—those who have undergone gene therapy enhancement. Perhaps new rules could specify just how much genetic alteration is legal. This is the brave new world that ethicists dread as a nightmare.

Actually, scenarios like this have long been anticipated. In 2003 the World Anti-Doping Agency, a group that helps maintain con-

The gene therapy techniques that offer such promise to people who are ill could possibly also be used to enhance athletic performance. This idea concerns ethicists, who warn about the effect on standards of fair competition.

sistent drug policies for sports organizations and governments, included gene doping on its list of banned substances. The agency defines *gene doping* as "the non-therapeutic use of genes, genetic elements and/or cells that have the capacity to enhance athletic performance."[27] Its appeal to athletes willing to cheat is that its use is hard to detect. A transgene—one transferred from one organism to another—and its expressed protein are virtually impossible to tell from their natural counterparts. Another factor is the relative success of gene therapy approaches that are targeted to muscle, which are just the type that tend to enhance physical performance in animal tests. Possible effects could include increased muscle size, heightened endurance, reduced pain reaction, and more rapid healing. Ethical worries about gene doping in sports, however, go far beyond concerns for the integrity of competition and fair play. Officials fear risks to the health and potentially the lives of athletes who might submit to such dangerously experimental treatments to gain an advantage on the field. Reckless use of gene therapy for such purposes, especially gene therapy on the germ line, could affect not only today's athletes but their children and grandchildren.

Compassion Versus Profit

A technology with the potential to cure diseases permanently and impact not only current lives but generations to come obviously has rosy financial prospects as well. One of the most common criticisms of gene therapy today is the enormous price for treatment. Glybera, the first gene therapy product approved for sale in Europe, has been called the most expensive drug in the world. In November 2014 it went on sale for 1 million euros ($1.1 million) per patient. Chiesi, the marketing partner of the Dutch company that makes Glybera, insists that the price is not excessive since patients can expect to be permanently cured. Because Glybera treats such a rare disorder—only an estimated four hundred to five hundred patients across Europe have the mutation that the drug addresses—its impact on health budgets should be limited. And supporters point out that such high prices are needed to compensate biotech firms for their large investment on research

Patenting Gene Therapy

Biotech companies spend millions of dollars developing and testing new drugs. To protect an investment and their ability to profit from it, these companies apply for government patents. A patent gives an inventor or company exclusive rights to market an invention for twenty years. Another firm or individual can use the invention to develop a product only by signing a licensing agreement with the patent holder. The process seems straightforward when applied to manufactured drugs. Problems arise, however, when the drug in question is a gene therapy treatment that includes human DNA. Can an edited sequence of a person's DNA be patented as a new invention? According to intellectual property attorney William L. Anthony, "Almost invariably, if I talk about patenting something that has to do with human beings, the first reaction is revulsion."

In general, polls show a public that is queasy about patenting DNA, which people associate with ownership of life's building blocks. Lawyers might explain that a patent does not involve ownership, only the right to exclusive use for a period of time. A tentative answer to this thorny question appeared in 2013 when the US Supreme Court ruled on the case *Association for Molecular Pathology v. Myriad Genetics*. The court decided that naturally occurring genes could not be patented, but it left open the possibility that an engineered gene as used in gene therapy might be patentable. Perhaps someday custom DNA will be available to shoppers as readily as aspirin or eyeglasses.

Quoted in Miriam Schulman, "Of SNPS, TRIPS, and Human Dignity: Ethics and Gene Patenting," Santa Clara University, 2014. www.scu.edu.

and development. Financial analysts say Glybera's launch may well set the benchmark for commercial gene therapy prices for the foreseeable future.

Financial considerations can also intrude on gene therapy in subtler ways. More than a decade ago, a company sought a gene therapy treatment for hair loss in chemotherapy patients. What at first seemed an admirable motive—alleviating the trauma of hair loss in seriously ill patients—was questioned when the focus of the company's research changed to treating ordinary male-pattern baldness. (The research never reached the product stage.) Critics tend to draw an ethical line between using gene therapy to address a disease or its effects and using it for some form of physical enhancement. As research proceeds, society may have to decide whether and to what extent gene therapy should be allowed for cosmetic changes as well as medicinal purposes. "The bottom line is that with the social pressures and the commercial pressures, doctors' hopes to restrict gene therapy to medical uses are simply a fantasy," says David King, the founder and director of the UK watchdog group Human Genetics Alert. "If we want to tackle this problem, we have to tackle that whole tendency in society not to accept any limits imposed by biology. But from where I'm standing it looks unlikely that we're going to stop this juggernaut. . . . The genie is now out of the bottle, and the only barrier left is at the germline."[28] Indeed, a future of narrowly tailored designer genes may be closer than most people think.

Chapter Four

Gene Therapy and Social Policy

Focus Questions

1. Do you think drug regulation in the United States should be affected by regulatory decisions in other nations? Why or why not?
2. The federal government has yet to approve a gene therapy product for sale in the United States. What effect, if any, does this fact have on gene therapy research?
3. What do you think is meant by the term *regulatory thaw*? Explain your answer.

"Just as the microscope and Bunsen burner are insufficient tools for modern genomics research, today's antiquated programs and policies governing the translation of research into public health benefits are not up to the task of bringing about the genomics age."

—Policy statement of the Genetics and Public Policy Center, Johns Hopkins University.

Genetics and Public Policy Center, "Overview: Our Genetic Future," 2010. www.dnapolicy.org.

In 2012, five-year-old Emily Whitehead was diagnosed with an aggressive form of leukemia. In her first round of chemotherapy—a treatment that is effective for most children with her disease—Emily got a deadly infection that almost cost her her legs. She suffered relapse twice during chemo, the last time while waiting for a bone marrow transplant. With no more options, Emily's parents turned to an experimental gene therapy treatment never before administered to a child. Doctors at the Children's Hospital of Philadelphia took blood from Emily, removed its white cells with a machine, and put the blood back. Next, scientists from the University of Pennsylvania used a vector made from modified HIV virus to reprogram the white blood cells to attack Emily's cancer. However, when the white cells were injected back into Emily's bloodstream, they began to attack her body in an out-of-control immune response. Swollen unrecognizably and suffering with a fever of 105°F (41°C), she was immediately placed in intensive care. Her parents were told her chances of survival were one in a thousand. Yet after receiving a drug for rheumatoid arthritis, Emily began to recover. Her immune system stopped attacking her healthy cells but continued to kill cancer cells.

As of early 2015, Emily was still in remission and remarkably healthy, taking piano lessons, and enjoying grade school. A number of older patients with the same type of leukemia have experienced similar results, with their cancer-fighting T cells remaining active in the bloodstream. Novartis, a large drug company, is so impressed that it has announced plans to market Emily's gene therapy treatment. "It really is a revolution," says Crystal Mackall of the National Cancer Institute. "This is going to open the door for all sorts of cell-based and gene therapy for all kinds of disease because it's going to demonstrate that it's economically viable."[29] Some observers, however, see more than a sudden breakthrough in making cancer-killing cells. They claim Emily's case is not a testimonial for America's policy toward gene therapy and other cutting-edge treatments, but an indictment.

remission

Abatement of the symptoms of a disease for a period.

Problems with Regulation
Critics point out that Emily is the first child in the United States to receive gene therapy treatment for cancer. Yet oncologists in China have been using gene therapy with cancer patients of all

ages for more than a decade. When Arthur Winiarski, an American businessman suffering from a fist-sized tumor and given only months to live, was denied gene therapy in the United States, he sought treatment in Beijing's Tongren Hospital. Under the care of Harvard-trained physician Niu Qi, Winiarski experienced complete remission. Gendicine, the drug he received, won approval from China's version of the FDA in 2003, but the US government has yet to approve the use of any experimental gene therapy drug. American patients who fail to gain admission to tightly controlled clinical tests are out of luck. Says political writer Ian Huyett:

> The Chinese have not left us in the dust because of their technological superiority. They have surpassed us because they are, apparently, less inclined to let life-saving technology languish in an abyss while their own people die. If Arthur Winiarski had not left the United States, he would be dead. Presumably, in the years between Winiarski's victory and [Emily] Whitehead's, many Americans who could have benefited from drugs like Gendicine did not leave the United States and are consequently dead.[30]

A growing number of patient advocates say individuals should have the right to volunteer for risky treatments when they have no other options. Parents of afflicted children also urge a more lenient policy of informed consent. Says the mother of a young child with an inherited brain disorder, "We don't have the luxury of waiting."[31]

Regulators respond that their main duty is to protect human subjects in clinical trials as well as the general public and the environment. And there is no doubt that gene therapy has drawn extra attention in this regard. Kenneth Cornetta, professor of molecular genetics at Indiana University, writes in a study on regulatory issues, "Public concerns regarding recombinant DNA technology led to additional levels of oversight which are unique to human gene therapy trials. The deaths of a normal volunteer and a gene therapy subject in the late 1990s led to an intensification of oversight."[32] Cornetta is referring, of course, to Jesse Gelsinger, the young trial subject whose death in 1999 remains the most divisive event in the technology's history. Because of what happened to Gelsinger, regulators have been more cautious in their approach to every aspect of gene therapy, from the design of clinical trials to the approval of products. Their caution can seem justified by statements from researchers such as James M. Wilson, who headed the Gelsinger study. "With what I know now, I wouldn't have proceeded with the study," Wilson says. "We were drawn into the simplicity of the concept. You just put the gene in."[33] Even though the European Union recently approved the gene therapy drug Glybera for sale, its regulators generally have proceeded with the same caution as their American counterparts. No one wants to be responsible for another tragedy, even if it means slowing the development of gene therapy to a crawl.

Emily Whitehead, pictured with her father in 2013, underwent an experimental gene therapy treatment after she was diagnosed with an aggressive form of leukemia in 2012. The seeming success of this therapy has given hope to other patients and encouraged scientists to continue their work.

Gene Therapy Regulation in the United States

The United States has no federal laws that cover gene therapy specifically. Federal health agencies have used older laws to address questions of genetic research. Federal regulation of so-called biologics—medical products made from living sources, from humans and animals to plants and microorganisms—dates to the 1902 Biologics Control Act. This resulted from a case in which tainted blood serum from a horse with tetanus caused the deaths of thirteen children being treated for diphtheria. In succeeding decades this law was employed to license drug products such as vaccines for smallpox and serums to protect against bacterial infections. The law sought to eliminate products that contained impure or inferior ingredients or made misleading claims. In 1938 Congress passed the Federal Food, Drug, and Cosmetic Act, which specified that a biological product be treated like a drug. Control of biologics remained under the National Institutes of Health (NIH) until 1972, when it passed to the FDA. By this time, genetic research was well underway, creating whole new categories of biologics. Old laws that predated discovery of the DNA double helix, such as the Federal Food, Drug, and Cosmetics Act and the Public Health Service Act, were thought sufficient for federal oversight of this new technology. Thus, instead of passing new laws, Congress authorized health officials to regulate the development of gene therapy and similar treatments. The result has been a confusing and often overlapping array of boards and agencies.

> **biologics**
>
> Medical products made from living sources, including humans, animals, plants, and microorganisms.

Much of this authority has fallen to the FDA, which has declared that gene therapy products are basically drugs. Or as the FDA website puts it, "Nucleic acids used for human gene therapy trials will be subject to the same requirements as other biological drugs."[34] In 1993 the FDA explained the legal basis for its authority to regulate gene therapy with a notice in the *Federal Register*, a daily paper that describes new government rules and regula-

Glybera and European Regulation of Gene Therapy

Much has been made of the European Union's 2012 approval of Glybera as the first gene therapy drug to be marketed legally in the West. Some reports depicted the European Medicines Agency (EMA) as surprisingly liberal in its decision, at least when compared with the American FDA, which has yet to approve any gene therapy treatment for sale. Yet a closer look at Glybera's arduous uphill struggle to win approval tells a different story. Mindful of the risks and failures that have plagued the technology, the EMA is essentially just as cautious as its American counterpart.

Glybera uses viral vectors to deliver a gene encoding a fat-processing enzyme that certain patients lack. The patients' rare inherited disorder causes them to accumulate so much fat in their blood after meals that the blood appears white rather than red. Fortunately, only a few hundred people suffer from the disease, making Glybera a narrowly targeted drug. Yet some experts still doubt whether Glybera is proven to be an effective treatment. They note that clinical trials involved only twenty-seven patients. The Committee for Medicinal Products for Human Use, which advises the EMA on approval of new drugs, three times rejected Glybera in the year before its final acceptance. The committee cited evidence of the drug causing inflammation of the pancreas. The committee reversed its decision only after it narrowed the group eligible for treatment to those with the most severe form of the disease. From the evidence, gene therapy still faces major hurdles in Europe.

tions. Actually, regulation of gene therapy is two pronged, involving products and research.

The FDA's focus is to ensure the quality and safety of gene therapy products, mainly through the Center for Biologics Evaluation and Research. A manufacturer seeking to market a gene therapy product in the United States must first inform the FDA of its plans. The manufacturer then can proceed with tests in the laboratory and on research animals. Before moving on to testing humans, the manufacturer must obtain a special permission exemption from the FDA, called an investigational new drug application. In the application, the manufacturer details how it will conduct the human trial (or protocol), what risks are involved, and how it intends to provide for patient safety. The manufacturer must also show that it has informed patients about potential risks and obtained their consent for the trial. A board of scientific and medical advisers studies the proposal and may suggest extra safeguards such as smaller doses for patients. The FDA retains authority to halt a trial at any point.

Regulation of gene therapy research, including clinical trials, is handled by the NIH. It is the NIH whose explicit policy bans all research on germ line (reproductive) cells in humans. While the NIH's authority over gene therapy research is legally limited to groups that receive federal funding, private institutions voluntarily follow these regulations as well. The Recombinant DNA Advisory Committee (RAC), established in 1974, has created detailed guidelines for gene therapy research, and all gene therapy clinical trials in the United States must also obtain RAC approval.

A biotech worker prepares a batch of smallpox vaccine. Smallpox vaccine is one of many drug products licensed under the Biologics Control Act, which strives to eliminate the use of impure and inferior ingredients in drugs.

A Slow Regulatory Thaw

Frustration with the alphabet soup of government regulatory agencies and the slow pace of progress has stymied many gene therapy researchers and biotech companies. "There was a whole chill on the field that lasted a couple of years," says Carl June, a researcher at the University of Pennsylvania, where the Gelsinger case occurred. "Everyone who was running a gene therapy trial was closed down until the FDA figured out new forms of oversight and additional safety criteria."[35] Others think gene therapy research was unfairly targeted due to sensational press coverage. According to R. Jude Samulski, director of the Gene Therapy Center at the University of North Carolina, "If you look at the positive results the field has had with retroviruses and the 'bubble boy' disease, anyone else who created a therapy with an 80 percent cure rate for an otherwise incurable disease would likely be judged a smashing success. . . . We brought undue scrutiny upon ourselves, and we're paying the price for it."[36] The price Samulski refers to is an FDA policy that many scientists believe is too restrictive on the number of clinical trials it approves, the number of patients in each trial, and the speed with which trials can proceed.

Breakthroughs with new vectors and treatment methods have reenergized gene therapy research in the past few years. These advances have helped bring about a slow regulatory thaw and an increase in the number of approved clinical trials. Yet scientists still see room for improvement. In December 2013 a panel of experts at the Institute of Medicine (IOM) at the National Academies advised government officials to ease off the brakes even more. The IOM panel recommended the RAC be phased out in its present form and replaced by a new committee dedicated to more streamlined reviews of trials. The panel also sought an end to redundant regulations and the filing of multiple trial plans for review, a frequent complaint among researchers. In making its recommendations, the panel noted that gene therapy has proved its worth, and its leaders have handled ethical issues responsibly. "Many of the original fears associated with gene transfer have not been borne out," according to the IOM report. The report also observes that "public perception has largely transitioned from negative to positive"[37] due

The CRISPR Debate

In a glitzy November 2014 ceremony reminiscent of the Oscars, biologists Jennifer Doudna and Emmanuelle Charpentier accepted the Breakthrough Prize for their pioneering work on CRISPR-Cas9, an amazing bacterial tool for editing strands of DNA. The women each received an award of $3 million, along with their newfound recognition among scientific peers. The awards emphasized the unique place CRISPR occupies in the field of gene therapy. Even though no CRISPR drug has yet been produced, it has been called the biggest breakthrough in biotechnology in more than forty years. And yet, with biotech companies scrambling for position, no one is quite sure who—if anyone—owns the invention.

Questions of ownership involve three brilliant scientists, three heavily financed new companies, six large universities, and reams of legal documents. One fact not in dispute is that in April 2014 Feng Zhang, a researcher at the Broad Institute at MIT and Harvard, obtained a US patent on CRISPR-Cas9 for Editas Medicine, the company he cofounded with Doudna. Meanwhile, Doudna left Editas for another company, taking her intellectual property claims on CRISPR with her. To further confuse the issue, Charpentier sold her own rights to a third company, CRISPR Therapeutics. Through all the legal turmoil, researchers are concentrating on what the technology can do. Some suggest that CRISPR, for all its exciting potential as a gene therapy tool, is actually easily reproducible and so is not worthy of a unique patent. "Things are happening fast," says Charpentier, "maybe a bit too fast."

Quoted in Antonio Regalado, "Who Owns the Biggest Biotech Discovery of the Century?," *MIT Technology Review*, December 4, 2014. www.technologyreview.com.

to the success of gene therapy in treating disorders such as blindness and hemophilia. With this in mind, the panel concluded that gene therapy should be regulated more like other cutting-edge medical technologies.

Federal officials' first reaction to the report was unenthusiastic. However, NIH director Francis S. Collins now seems to agree with the report's findings. "I have considered the IOM report carefully and have decided to accept the IOM committee recommendations on RAC review of gene therapy research," Collins writes.

"Given the progress in the field, I am confident that . . . a stream-lined process will reduce duplication and delays in getting gene transfer trials initiated."[38] Gene therapy researchers hope this new mind-set displayed by an important regulator leads to more numerous and more rapid approvals for clinical trials.

Biotech Companies' Gamble

Given the often glacial pace of research, plus the fact that after decades the FDA has yet to approve a single gene therapy product for sale in the United States, biotech companies that invest in the technology are making a large gamble. Often a company's bet involves tens of millions of dollars in research and development funds. Yet despite the financial risks, more companies are responding to what appears to be an easing of regulations in order

New treatment options based on gene transfer are created in the laboratory of this biotechnology company. Biotech companies spend tens of millions of dollars on research and development of various products.

to jump back into the gene therapy business. A good example is Editas Medicine, a start-up that has obtained $43 million in venture capital to pursue the CRISPR gene-editing technology. The financiers and scientists behind Editas are not satisfied with a cautious approach, preferring instead to swing for the fences. "The first thing we look at is the unmet need," says Editas interim president Kevin Bitterman.

"This is potentially such a transformational technology, it's less exciting for us to go after an area where there's already therapy and we can potentially make it slightly better. . . . We want to go after areas where there's truly no other option."[39] As proof of its optimism, Editas planned to add up to thirty new scientific staff members in 2014.

Even more promising is news that one of the world's largest drug companies is plunging into gene therapy. Late in 2014 Pfizer signed a deal with Spark Therapeutics, a small biotech start-up, to help it win FDA approval for a cutting-edge treatment for hemophilia B. Spark has already obtained the FDA's coveted breakthrough-therapy status for its gene therapy treatment of night blindness. Spark, a company that emerged from research at Children's Hospital of Philadelphia, hopes to work closely with FDA officials to get marketable products approved. Such confidence once would have seemed merely naive, but now it is shared by several powerhouse companies in the drug field, including Novartis, which plans to market the leukemia treatment that saved Emily Whitehead's life. Some of the companies are already planning their own gene therapy divisions. Experts predict that these big players—with their big money—will finally overcome the regulatory hurdles and establish gene therapy as an accepted medical tool worldwide.

Chapter Five

The Future of Gene Therapy

Focus Questions

1. How do you think research scientists working on gene therapy thirty years ago would view the landscape for gene therapy today? Explain your answer.
2. Should gene therapy treatment for diseases such as sickle-cell anemia and Parkinson's disease be made available to any American who has the disorder? Why or why not?
3. Do you think people with debilitating conditions such as inherited obesity or blindness should be required to have gene therapy treatment? Why or why not?

"A lot of [gene therapy's future] will boil down to what society says a human life is worth. What is it worth to take a debilitated person and turn them into a functioning person who can contribute more to society? That's a fundamental, big question."

—Barrie Carter, vice president of gene therapy at BioMarin Pharmaceutical.

Quoted in Luke Timmerman, "Gene Therapy Lurches Ahead, Sees Thorny Future Questions on Price," Xconomy, January 27, 2014. www.xconomy.com.

On January 17, 1994, the cover of *Time* magazine trumpeted the words "Genetics: The Future Is Now."[40] The public understandably expected miracle cures from new technologies such as gene therapy. When these hopes did not materialize at once, and clinical trials proved deadly in certain widely reported cases, many wrote off the technology as a failure. More than twenty years later the future predicted by *Time* and many scientists and physicians has still not arrived. Aside from some important breakthroughs, promising as they are, gene therapy remains a work in progress. When reading stories about the exciting potential of gene therapy today, nonexperts might be excused for rolling their eyes and saying they have heard all this before. Yet gene therapy researchers do seem on the verge of success on many different fronts. The sheer variety of approaches to the technology promises to bring surprising solutions to thorny problems. An actual gene therapy product is being sold in Europe, and the approval of American products seems imminent. Perhaps for gene therapy, the future—at last—*is* now.

Stem Cells and Gene Therapy

One of the newest approaches to gene therapy modifies stem cells with replacement genes. The method shows huge promise in treating sickle-cell anemia, a hereditary condition that afflicts more than ninety thousand people in the United States alone. The disease causes the body to form red blood cells shaped like the crescent blade of a sickle, instead of the normal disc shape.

> **stem cells**
>
> Undifferentiated biological cells with the ability to divide or self-renew indefinitely.

The stiff and sticky sickle cells can block blood flow to vessels leading to the limbs and organs. This can result in chronic pain, organ damage, and risk of infection. Researchers at the University of California–Los Angeles (UCLA) Broad Center of Regenerative Medicine and Stem Cell Research are testing a treatment for sickle-cell anemia that combines stem cells and gene therapy. Stem cells are a type of undifferentiated cell found in many parts of the body. They are like all-purpose recruits, able to form specialized cells that divide and renew themselves indefinitely. Dr. Donald Kohn and his team at UCLA hope to introduce an anti–sickle-cell gene into the patient's own blood stem cells, which are found in

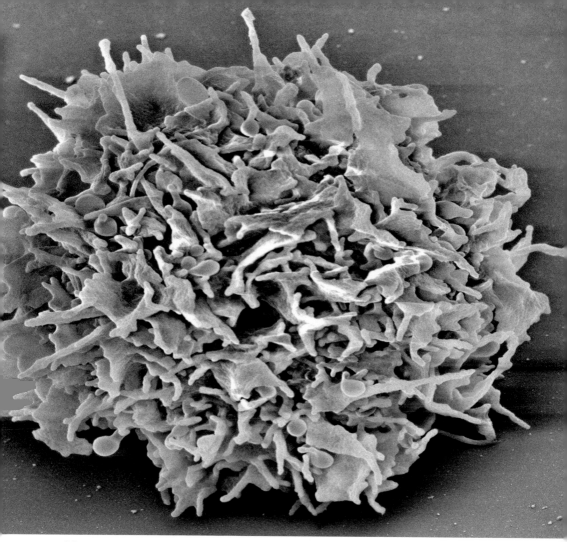

A bone marrow stem cell can be seen in this colored scanning electron micrograph. Researchers are testing a treatment for sickle-cell anemia that relies on stem cells found in the patient's own bone marrow.

bone marrow. The hope is that the treated blood cells will then manufacture healthy red blood cells without the sickle shapes. Sickle-cell anemia seems an ideal candidate for gene therapy since blood stem cells are the only cells that need the added gene. So far treatments have been restricted to a small number of patients with severe symptoms, but results are promising.

Another target of research using stem cells with gene therapy is heart disease. This condition, which is the number one cause of death in the United States, is usually the result of an enlarged heart or poor blood supply due to clogged arteries. It often leads

A Tiny Approach That Looms Large

One of the challenges of gene therapy is precisely targeting the location necessary to deliver replacement genes and have them express the needed function. A new approach enlists tiny nanoparticle robots to serve as gene messengers. Researchers at the California Institute of Technology in Pasadena have combined gene therapy and nanotechnology—the science of minuscule things—to treat tumors in cancer patients. The method is called RNA interference, and it uses RNA (ribonucleic acid) as a chemical messenger to switch off genes that manufacture disease-causing proteins in cancer. To deliver the RNA to tumor cells, the scientists fashioned microscopic polymer robots that are covered with a protein called transferrin. The tiny robots hunt for a receptor that lets them into cancer cells, where they release RNA to block troublesome genes. "In the particle itself, we've built what we call a chemical sensor," says Mark Davis, the study's leader. "When it recognizes that it's gone inside the cell, it says OK, now it's time to disassemble and give off the RNA."

Scientists at the Tokyo Institute of Technology have added an extra wrinkle to the nano-based approach to gene therapy. Their so-called nanomachines for delivering replacement genes are light controlled. The tiny messengers release their genetic payload only when activated by light, enabling the desired cells to be targeted with pinpoint timing and accuracy. Japanese researchers claim the method is one hundred times more efficient than other gene-delivery techniques.

Quoted in Julie Steenhuysen, "Nanotech Robots Deliver Gene Therapy Through Blood," Reuters, March 21, 2010. www.reuters.com.

to heart attack and severe damage to the heart muscle. Medical experts have long assumed heart muscle cells cannot regenerate. "People thought that the same heart you had as a young child, you had as an old man or woman as well,"[41] says Antonis Hatzopoulos, associate professor of medicine at Vanderbilt University. Now researchers from Icahn School of Medicine at Mount Sinai Hospital in New York City are trying to repair and regenerate injured heart tissue by injecting stem cells directly into damaged heart muscle following a heart attack. Early tests indicate that the so-called stem cell factor can be delivered via gene therapy to reduce the death of heart muscle cells and heart tissue scarring. The stem cells seem to enlist nearby cells in the heart to revive and improve heart function. "It is clear that the expression of the stem cell factor gene results in the generation of specific signals to neighboring cells in the damaged heart resulting in improved outcomes at the molecular, cellular, and organ level," says Roger J. Hajjar, director of the Cardiovascular Research Center at Mount Sinai Hospital and senior author of the study. "There is evidence that recruiting this small group of stem cells to the heart could be the basis of novel therapies for . . . advanced heart failure."[42] Overall, stem cells hold exciting possibilities for future use in gene therapy. Their ability to self-renew means that the number of gene therapy treatments can be reduced, with some treatments requiring no second administration at all.

Gene Therapy as a Virtual Pacemaker

Another way gene therapy may soon aid heart patients is by training heart cells to act as pacemakers. Some people suffer from a condition called heart block, in which the electrical signal that controls the heart's rhythm is slowed or interrupted as it moves through the heart. This can cause an abnormal heart rhythm, leading to drowsiness or in extreme cases cardiac arrest. Irregular heartbeat can occur even in fetal development. A healthy heart employs a few thousand cells that act as pacemakers and regulate the electrical pulses that control heart rate. Currently, people who have an abnormal heart rhythm from heart block can receive a mechanical pacemaker that corrects the problem. Each year more than three hundred thousand patients in the United States have pacemakers implanted. The device must be replaced after about seven years, and the surgery can lead to complications such as infection. Irregular heartbeat is a particularly difficult problem in prenatal hearts.

pacemaker

A device that regulates the rhythm of the heart.

Today, researchers at Cedars-Sinai Heart Institute in Los Angeles are testing ways to reprogram heart muscle cells using gene therapy. Institute director Eduardo Marbán and his team selected twelve pigs and injected half of them with a modified virus containing a gene called TBX18 and half with a placebo. The gene was delivered to an area in each pig's heart no larger than a peppercorn. The targeted cells serve as a metronome when healthy, firing electric impulses that regulate the heart's rhythm. The new gene reprograms dormant heart muscle cells to send the signals. After eight days, the pigs that received the new gene had significantly higher heart rates than those in the control group. Although the effectiveness dropped off after two weeks—the pigs' immune systems began to reject the virus—Marbán and his team were encouraged. "We have been able, for the first time, to create a biological pacemaker using minimally invasive methods," says Marbán, "and to show that the new pacemaker suffices to support the demands of daily life."[43] Marbán thinks the approach could be used in coming years with in utero babies who have congenital heart defects and obviously cannot be fitted with a pacemaker. The hope is that gene therapy might introduce a pacemaker effect before birth that takes hold and becomes permanent.

Promising Treatment for Parkinson's Disease

Experts on gene therapy often project a future of wonderful new treatments based on the technology. But Nicholas Mazarakis knows how unreliable such predictions can be and how difficult it is to develop an idea into an actual solution for patients. Mazarakis, a leading molecular neuroscientist at Imperial College London, first devised a gene therapy treatment for Parkinson's disease while working at the biotech company Oxford BioMedica in 1997. In January 2014, after sixteen years of tenacious labor, results of the first tests on humans were finally published. Mazarakis might be forgiven for shaking his head at people who proclaim clear skies ahead for gene therapy. He has lived through the constant highs and lows, the premature certainties and sudden setbacks that characterize research in this area. Now with such promising results made public, Mazarakis can take a deep breath. "It's taken a long time to get to this point," he says. "We've fought all the way. People are hesitant to accept it as it's so dramatic."[44]

Parkinson's disease is a neurological disorder that affects about 5 million people worldwide. The condition is the result of loss of nerve cells in a certain part of the brain, leading to a reduced level of the brain chemical dopamine. Once 80 percent of these nerve cells are lost, patients begin to experience severe physical symptoms. These include involuntary shaking, muscle stiffness, and slow movements in general. Sufferers are finally unable to perform everyday tasks such as dressing, cooking, and household chores.

dopamine
A brain chemical that serves as a neurotransmitter and regulates the body's movement, among many other actions.

Many gene therapies have been proposed to treat Parkinson's, but Mazarakis's strategy is unique. He delivers to patients three genes that code for enzymes that make dopamine. The viral vector is a hollowed-out lentivirus, a virus much like HIV that has a long incubation period and can also deliver large amounts of genetic information. The genes enter the striatum, a part of the brain that regulates movement, where they stimulate production of dopamine to counter the patient's deficiency. The treatment, called ProSavin, seems to be an improvement on current drugs whose effects are only temporary. The last resort for Parkinson's sufferers has been deep brain stimulation, in which patients submit to wires attached to the brain. Gene therapy, with its promise of extended relief, represents a much more palatable option. And so far the results of human trials have impressed the medical community. Mazarakis is confident that human subjects will show the remarkable improvement he witnessed in a group of dopamine-deficient monkeys that received the genes several years ago. At first the animals could barely move, but following treatment they were able to climb their cages freely.

Targeting Obesity

A study involving rats and mice on a high-fat diet may one day lead to gene therapy treatments for obesity. Recent surveys in the United States suggest that more than one-third of American adults are obese, and the condition leads to all sorts of related health problems, including hypertension, heart and liver disease, and diabetes. Estimated annual medical costs to treat obese patients in the United States are more than $150 billion. With these statistics in mind, researchers are urgently seeking new therapies to combat what is becoming a worldwide epidemic. They hope experiments on chubby rodents today will result in tomorrow's breakthrough treatments.

Obesity is a growing problem in the United States. Studies currently under way might one day lead to gene therapy treatments for obesity.

In recent years scientists discovered that the adipose tissue, or fat tissue, in individuals of a healthy weight secretes a protein that acts to protect the body in several ways. The protein, called adiponectin, helps break down fat, controls glucose levels, and regulates appetite. Apparently, as people gain too much weight and their fat cells enlarge, production of the healthy protein shuts down. "We haven't seen this amount of fat before," says Jason Dyck, a researcher at the University of Alberta in Canada, "so for some reason when the fat cells get to a certain size, they just stop secreting this protective hormone."[45] Dyck is working with colleagues on a gene therapy treatment that restores adiponectin to obese patients by prompting muscle cells to resume making the protein. Tests on rodents that had been fed a diet high in fat and sugar showed remarkable improvement, as the restored protein not only helped suppress appetite but also signaled the body to burn more energy. Dyck says he is not sure whether the mice become more active because they are thinner or become thinner as they grow more active. Either way, the therapy has had a positive effect.

Dyck hopes that gene therapy will gain acceptance as treatment for more everyday conditions like obesity and not just as a last-ditch treatment for life-threatening diseases. "If you have terminal cancer, researchers will take high risk gene therapy approaches and hope they can save lives that way," he says. "With obesity a lot of people don't see it in those terms as of yet, even though it's responsible for so many different diseases. But until it's considered a serious disease it's not going to be treated aggressively with gene therapy."[46]

Prolonging Life Span and the Road Ahead

The ultimate everyday ailment that afflicts every human being is the aging process. Even here scientists predict a role for gene therapy in slowing or perhaps reversing the ravages of age. Some of the competing claims have the dubious ring of late-night infomercials. The website for the Institute for Ethics & Emerging Technologies boasts of having found eleven genes that hold the most promise for extending life. "We will manipulate not a single gene, but several aging mechanisms simultaneously," declares the institute. "As a result, we will develop a comprehensive treatment that will not only dramatically extend lifespan, but will also prevent the decrepitude [frailty due to aging] of the body."[47]

Other researchers take a more measured approach yet still offer amazing possibilities. Scientists have found that calorie restrictions and healthful eating habits can promote the expression of health-promoting genes and limit the work of disease-promoting

A New Focus for Gene Therapy

Eyesight is universally seen as a precious commodity. So the ability of gene therapy to improve eyesight or prevent blindness may go a long way toward helping the technology gain acceptance in the future. Robert MacLaren, a professor of ophthalmology at Oxford University, recently concluded tests of a gene therapy treatment on a rare inherited eye disease called choroideremia. Published results were so positive that MacLaren and his team think the treatment may one day be used on more common causes of blindness.

Tests began in 2012 on Jonathan Wyatt, whose vision had become a blur due to the disorder. Wyatt, now sixty-five, received injection of an AAV vector containing a working copy of the defective gene that causes choroideremia. The vector was delivered directly to Wyatt's retinas. His improvement was immediate. "The very next day I saw a mobile phone and I said 'I can read the digits!'" says Wyatt. "I hadn't been able to read the digits on a mobile phone for five years."

Since then five more patients have received the treatment, and all report improved eyesight. MacLaren and his team think the treatment could last a lifetime, since it targets neuron photoreceptors that do not die out. Nevertheless, long-term results remain in question. One key to effective treatment is getting to the cells before they are completely destroyed. The next step is to figure out how to regenerate those lost cells. For now though, Jonathan Wyatt is happy to see the results of gene therapy.

Quoted in Abigail Beall, "Gene Therapy Restores Sight in People with Eye Disease," *New Scientist*, January 16, 2014. www.newscientist.com.

genes. Studies of yeast show that by switching off two particular aging genes, the life span of yeast is extended. Researchers at Tel Aviv University's Blavatnik School of Computer Science identified the aging genes in yeast using complex mathematical algorithms and hope to do the same with mice. Once identified, genes associated with the aging process could perhaps be reengineered with gene therapy from a diseased state into a healthy one. Scientists at the Spanish National Cancer Research Centre have lengthened a mouse's life span by inducing cells to express telomerase, an enzyme that can slow the biological clock. Maybe someday people will check into gene therapy clinics periodically to give their antiaging genes a boost.

algorithm

A procedure or formula for solving a problem.

Society's attitude toward gene therapy is assumed to be positive, although polls and surveys on the topic are years out of date. Pollsters, like politicians, seem reluctant to tackle the subject head-on. Meanwhile, the future for gene therapy remains bright. The number of clinical trials in the United States and around the world continues to increase, new approaches show great promise, and approval for new gene therapy products appears to be imminent. Changing the human genome at the germ line—and affecting generations to come—is still too risky and controversial to gain support beyond a few venturesome scientists. And regulators continue to focus on patient safety in light of past mistakes. Yet the lifesaving potential of gene therapy is best described by James D. Watson's words: "We used to think that our fate was in our stars. Now we know that, in large measure, our fate is in our genes."[48]

Source Notes

Introduction: A Promising Success

1. Quoted in Linda Geddes, "'Bubble Kid' Success Puts Gene Therapy Back on Track," *New Scientist*, October 30, 2013. www.newscientist.com.

2. Quoted in James Preston, "Baby Nina Astounds Doctors After Pioneering Gene Therapy," *Maidenhead Advertiser* (Maidenhead, England), January 17, 2014. www.maidenhead-advertiser.co.uk.

3. Quoted in Luke Timmerman, "Gene Therapy Lurches Ahead, Sees Thorny Future Questions on Price," Xconomy, January 27, 2014. www.xconomy.com.

Chapter One: The Origin of Gene Therapy

4. Quoted in National Library of Medicine, "The Francis Crick Papers: The Discovery of the Double Helix, 1951–1953." http://profiles.nlm.nih.gov.

5. Quoted in Cold Spring Harbor Oral History Collection, "Hamilton Smith on the Search for Restriction Enzymes at Hopkins," March 3, 2006. http://library.cshl.edu.

6. Quoted in DNA Learning Center, "The Origin and Utility of Recombinant DNA, Paul Berg." www.dnalc.org.

7. Ramez Naam, "More than Human," *New York Times*, July 3, 2005. www.nytimes.com.

8. Quoted in *Scientific American Frontiers*, "Hope for Gene Therapy," PBS. www.pbs.org.

9. Quoted in Liz Bowie, "Gene Therapy Used for First Time on Brain Tumor," *Baltimore* (MD) *Sun*, December 9, 1992. http://articles.baltimoresun.com.

Chapter Two: Balancing Safety and Research

10. Quoted in Everett Mendelsohn, "The Eugenic Temptation," *Harvard Magazine*, March–April 2000. http://harvardmagazine.com.

11. Quoted in Sheryl Gay Stolberg, "The Biotech Death of Jesse Gelsinger," *New York Times*, November 28, 1999. www.nytimes.com.

12. Donna Shalala, "Protecting Research Subjects—What Must Be Done," *New England Journal of Medicine*, September 14, 2000. www.nejm.org.
13. Quoted in Barbara Sibbald, "Death but One Unintended Consequence of Gene-Therapy Trial," *Canadian Medical Association Journal*, May 29, 2001. www.cmaj.ca.
14. Quoted in Jef Akst, "Targeting DNA," *Scientist*, June 1, 2012. www.the-scientist.com.
15. Jay P. Siegel, "Testimony on 'Gene Therapy: Is There Oversight for Patient Safety?,'" Assistant Secretary for Legislation, Department of Health & Human Services, February 2, 2000. www.hhs.gov.
16. Quoted in Carl Zimmer, "The Fall and Rise of Gene Therapy," *Wired*, August 13, 2013. www.wired.com.
17. Quoted in Zimmer, "The Fall and Rise of Gene Therapy."
18. Quoted in Akst, "Targeting DNA."
19. Quoted in European Medicines Agency, "European Medicines Agency Recommends First Gene Therapy for Approval," July 20, 2012. www.ema.europa.eu.
20. Quoted in Nuala Moran, "Glybera Gains Official EMA Nod as First Gene Therapy," BioWorld, 2014. www.bioworld.com.

Chapter Three: The Ethics of Gene Therapy

21. Quoted in Ben Spencer, "'Jaw-Dropping' New Form of Gene Therapy Could Allow Scientists to Modify Human DNA and Transform Treatment of Incurable Genetic Diseases," *Daily Mail* (London), November 6, 2013. www.dailymail.co.uk.
22. Quoted in Robert Buderi, "Controversy Surrounds Gene Therapy Effort," *Scientist*, January 23, 1989. www.the-scientist.com.
23. Church of Scotland: Society, Religion and Technology Project, "Moral and Ethical Issues in Gene Therapy," April 14, 2010. www.srtp.org.uk.
24. Quoted in N. Schichor, J. Simonet, and C. Canano, "Should We Allow Genetic Engineering? A Public Policy Analysis of Germline Enhancement," in *Developmental Biology*, 10th ed., ed. Scott F. Gilbert. Sunderland, MA: Sinauer Associates, 2013. http://10e.devbio.com.

25. Schichor et al., "Should We Allow Genetic Engineering? A Public Policy Analysis of Germline Enhancement."
26. *Nature*, "Gene Therapy and the Germline," 1999. www.nature.com.
27. Quoted in Anna Baoutina, Ian E. Alexander, John E. J. Rasko, and Kerry R. Emslie, "Potential Use of Gene Transfer in Athletic Performance Enhancement," *Molecular Therapy*, August 7, 2007. www.nature.com.
28. David King, "Social Issues Raised by Gene Therapy," Human Genetics Alert, May 6, 1997. www.hgalert.org.

Chapter Four: Gene Therapy and Social Policy

29. Quoted in Matthew Herper, "Is This How We'll Cure Cancer?," *Forbes*, May 26, 2014. www.forbes.com.
30. Ian Huyett, "Regulation Kills: The FDA's War on Gene Therapy," FreedomWorks, June 4, 2013. www.freedomworks.org.
31. Quoted in Rick Weiss, "Caution over Gene Therapy Puts Hopes on Hold," *Washington Post*, March 7, 2000. www.washingtonpost.com.
32. Kenneth Cornetta, "Regulatory Issues in Human Gene Therapy," National Center for Biotechnology Information, July–August 2003. www.ncbi.nlm.nih.gov.
33. Quoted in Patricia Fitzpatrick Dimond, "The RAC: Still Needed After All These Years?," *Genetic Engineering & Biotechnology News*, May 28, 2014. http://genengnews.com.
34. Quoted in Genetics & Public Policy Center, "Human Genetic Modification: Federal Food, Drug and Cosmetic Act," 2010. www.dnapolicy.org.
35. Quoted in John Carroll, "Gene Therapy: Science in Slow Motion," *Biotechnology Healthcare*, February 2007. www.ncbi.nlm.nih.gov.
36. Quoted in Carroll, "Gene Therapy."
37. Quoted in Eliot Marshall, "United States Should End Gene Therapy Review Panel, Study Says," *Science*, December 5, 2013. http://news.sciencemag.org.
38. Quoted in National Institutes of Health, "Statement by the NIH Director on the IOM Report Addressing the Role of the Re-

combinant DNA Advisory Committee in Oversight of Clinical Gene Transfer Protocols," May 22, 2014. www.nih.gov.

39. Quoted in Aaron Krol, "Gene Therapy's Next Generation," *Bio-IT World*, January 29, 2014. www.bio-itworld.com.

Chapter Five: The Future of Gene Therapy

40. *Time*, "Genetics: The Future Is Now," January 17, 1994.

41. Quoted in ScienceDaily, "Coronary Arteries Hold Heart-Regenerating Cells," August 20, 2014. www.sciencedaily .com.

42. Quoted in Mount Sinai Hospital, "Delivery of Stem Cells into Heart Muscle After Heart Attack May Enhance Cardiac Repair and Reverse Injury," November 19, 2014. www.mountsinai .org.

43. Quoted in Caelainn Hogan, "Gene Therapy Can Reprogram Heart Muscle Cells to Act as Biological Pacemaker," *Washington Post*, July 16, 2014. www.washingtonpost.com.

44. Quoted in Sam Wong, "Gene Therapy for Parkinson's Disease Yields Promising Results in First Patients," Imperial College London, January 10, 2014. www3.imperial.ac.uk.

45. Quoted in Liz Brown, "Gene Therapy Injections: Future Obesity Cure?," *Toronto* (ON) *Metro*, May 14, 2014. http:// metronews.ca.

46. Quoted in Brown, "Gene Therapy Injections."

47. Maria Konovalenko, "Longevity Therapy Is the Best Way to Defeat Aging," Institute for Ethics & Emerging Technologies, September 23, 2014. http://ieet.org.

48. Quoted in Leon Jaroff, "The Gene Hunt," *Time*, March 20, 1989. www.time.com.

Books

Francis S. Collins, *The Language of Life: DNA and the Revolution in Personalized Medicine*. New York: HarperCollins, 2010.

David Epstein, *The Sports Gene: Inside the Science of Extraordinary Athletic Performance*. New York: Penguin, 2014.

Roland W. Herzog and Sergei Zolotukhin, *A Guide to Human Gene Therapy*. Hackensack, NJ: World Scientific, 2010.

Ricki Lewis, *The Forever Fix: Gene Therapy and the Boy Who Saved It*. New York: St. Martin's, 2013.

Ramez Naam, *More than Human: Embracing the Promise of Biological Enhancement*. New York: Broadway, 2010.

Internet Sources

Pam Belluck, "Gene Therapy Is Used to Adjust Pigs' Heartbeat," *New York Times*, July 16, 2014. www.nytimes.com /2014/07/17/health/gene-therapy-used-to-create-biological -pacemaker-in-pigs.html.

Francie Diep, "The Science and Troubling Ethics of Gene Therapy," *Popular Science*, September 4, 2013. www.popsci .com/science/article/2013-09/science-and-troubling-ethics -gene-therapy.

R. Alan Leo, "The Gene Therapy Renaissance," Harvard Medical School, April 18, 2013. http://hms.harvard.edu/news /gene-therapy-renaissance-4-18-13.

Susan Young Rojahn, "When Will Gene Therapy Come to the U.S.?," *MIT Technology Review*, September 30, 2013. http:// hms.harvard.edu/news/gene-therapy-renaissance-4-18-13.

Melinda Wenner, "Gene Therapy: An Interview with an Unfortunate Pioneer," *Scientific American*, August 17, 2009. www .scientificamerican.com/article/gene-therapy-an-interview/.

Websites

Gene Therapy Net (www.genetherapynet.com). This website features a wide variety of articles about the latest developments in gene therapy technology.

National Human Genome Research Institute (www.genome .gov). This website, sponsored by the National Institutes of Health, includes informative discussions of topics such as germ line gene transfer and gene therapy for genetic enhancement.

ScienceDaily (www.sciencedaily.com). This website is a good source of stories on cutting-edge gene therapy.

US Food and Drug Administration (www.fda.gov). This website includes articles and features on the history and current state of regulating biological products, including gene therapy.

Wired (www.wired.com). This website provides a look at the work of science and technology, including gene therapy, with in-depth stories for the general reader.